Introduction

Everywhere you look in quilt shops and online you see wonderful morsels of 5" squares of fabric called charms. They may have other names as well, but all charm packs contain 5" precut squares of coordinating fabrics. If you really dig into the creative possibilities of these bundles you will be amazed. They're both fun and easy to work with if you have the patterns to support their use.

Just Charm Quilts is a collection of fun but easy patterns with great style all made with 5" charms. There are projects using several packages or as few as one package, and some you can make using leftovers from previous projects. Each pattern was designed specifically to use 5" squares to create stylish quilted projects. You'll find everything from bed quilts to hot pads, and ideas for so much more. If you're looking for charm inspiration, you've found it!

Enjoy!

Table of Contents

Charm Plus

You'll be amazed at how far a couple of charm packs can be stretched with this pattern. Small amounts of fabric can make a big statement.

Design by Bev Getschel
Quilted by Lynette Gelling

Skill Level

Confident Beginner

Finished Size

Quilt Size: 67⅝" x 83¼"

Block Size: 9" x 9"

Number of Blocks: 32

Materials

- 32 matching pairs 5" precut squares
- 8 assorted 5" precut squares
- ⅔ yard black print
- 4½ yards cream solid
- Backing to size
- Batting to size
- Thread
- Basic sewing tools and supplies

Project Notes

Read all instructions before beginning this project.

Stitch right sides together using a ¼" seam allowance unless otherwise specified.

Materials and cutting lists assume 41" of usable fabric width for yardage.

Cutting

From 32 matching pairs precut squares:

- From each pair, cut 4 (2½" x 5") A rectangles.

From 8 assorted precut squares:

- Cut 30 (2½") C squares.

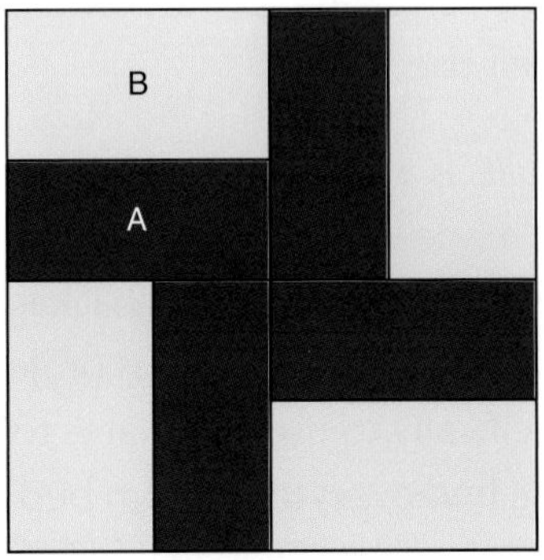

Charm
9" x 9" Finished Block
Make 32

From black print:

- Cut 8 (2¼" by fabric width) binding strips.

From cream solid:

- Cut 2 (16⅞" by fabric width) strips.
  Subcut strips into 4 (16⅞") M squares and 2 (7¼") N squares. Cut each M square on both diagonals to make 16 M triangles; discard 2. Cut each N square in half on 1 diagonal to make 4 N triangles.
- Cut 2 (9½" by fabric width) strips.
  Subcut strips into 26 (2½" x 9½") I rectangles.
- Cut 10 (5" by fabric width) strips.
  Subcut strips into 128 (3" x 5") B rectangles.
- Cut 2 (2½" by fabric width) strips.
  Subcut strips into 30 (2½") D squares.
- Cut 4 (2½" by fabric width) strips.
  Subcut strips into 2 each (2½" x 32½") E strips and (2½" x 28½") G strips.
- Cut 5 (4½" by fabric width) strips.
  Subcut 2 strips into 2 (4½" x 40⅛") H strips. Set aside 3 remaining strips for F.
- Cut 5 (2½" by fabric width) J/K/L strips.

Completing the Blocks

1. To make one block, select four matching A rectangles and four B rectangles.

2. Sew one each A and B rectangle together to make an A-B unit as shown in Figure 1; press. Repeat to make a total of four A-B units; press.

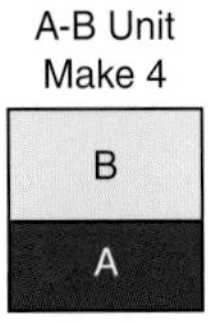

Figure 1

3. Referring to Figure 2, arrange and sew A-B units into two rows; press. Sew rows together to complete one Charm block; press.

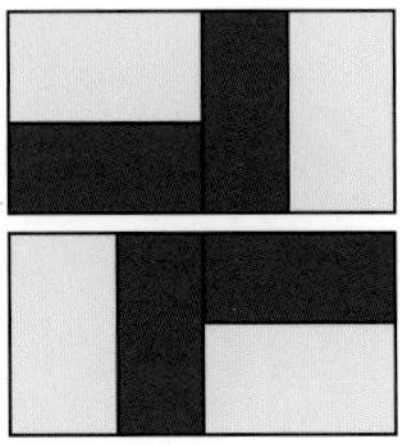

Figure 2

4. Repeat steps 1–3 to make a total of 32 Charm blocks.

Completing the Quilt

Refer to the Assembly Diagram for positioning of blocks, strips and borders.

1. Sew J/K/L strips together on the short ends to make one long strip; press. Subcut strip into two each 2½" x 31½" J strips and 2½" x 53½" K strips, and one 2½" x 64½" L strip.

2. Arrange and alternately stitch six Charm blocks and five I rectangles into a row; press. Repeat to make a second row.

3. Sew L strip between the two rows to complete a sashed two-row section; press.

4. Arrange and sew one each Charm block, I rectangle and M and N triangle together to form a corner unit; press. Repeat to make a second corner unit.

5. Sew a corner unit to each end of sashed two-row section to complete the center strip; press.

6. Arrange and alternately stitch five Charm blocks and four I rectangles into a five-block row; press. Repeat to make a second five-block row.

7. Sew a K strip to one long side of each five-block row; press. Sew an M triangle to each end of pieced rows to complete two K rows; press.

8. Arrange and alternately stitch three Charm blocks and two I rectangles into a three-block row; press. Repeat to make a second three-block row.

9. Sew a J strip to one long side of each three-block row; press. Sew an M triangle to each end of pieced rows to make two J rows; press.

10. Sew an I rectangle and N triangle to opposite sides of a Charm block; press. Sew M triangles to remaining sides to make a corner unit; press. Repeat to make a second corner unit.

11. Sew corner units, J and K rows and center strip together to complete the quilt center; press.

12. Alternately stitch seven each C and D squares as shown in Figure 3 to make a short border row. Repeat to make a second short border row.

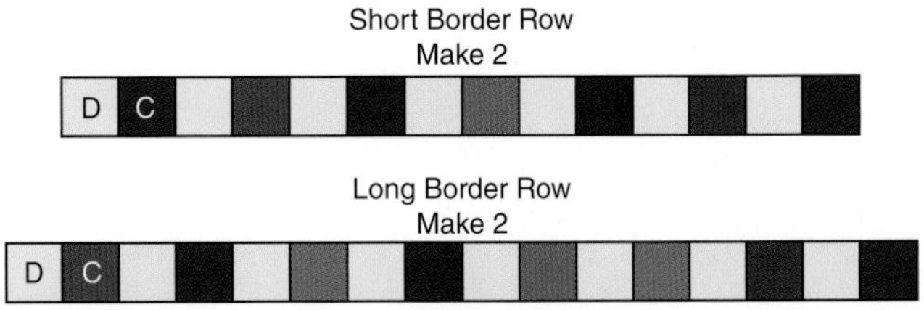

Figure 3

13. Again referring to Figure 3, alternately sew eight each C and D squares to make a long border row. Repeat to make a second long border row.

14. Sew F strips together on the short ends to make one long strip; press. Subcut strip into two 4½" x 43¾" F strips.

15. Sew an E strip to one long side of a long border row as shown in Figure 4; press. Sew an F strip to left end to make a side border unit; press. Repeat to make a second side border unit.

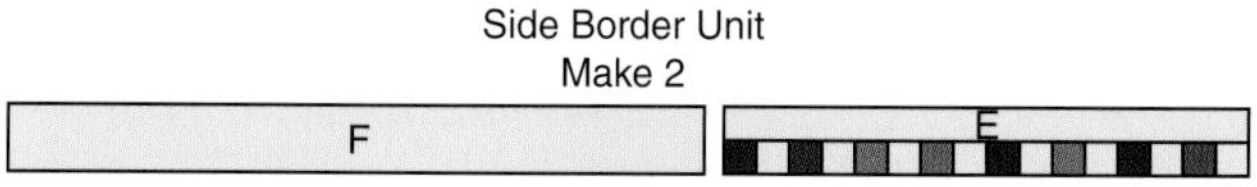

Figure 4

16. Sew a G strip to one long side of a short border row as shown in Figure 5; press. Sew an H strip to right end to make the top border unit; press. Repeat to make the bottom border unit.

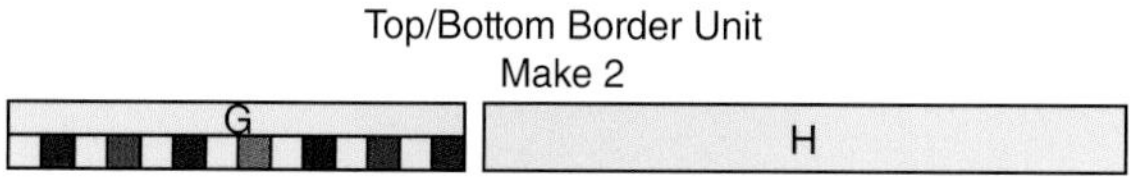

Figure 5

17. Stitch side border units to opposite sides of pieced center; press. Stitch top and bottom border units in place to complete the quilt top; press.

18. Layer, quilt and bind referring to Quilting Basics on page 45. ●

Charm Plus
Assembly Diagram $67^{5}/_{8}$" x $83^{1}/_{4}$"

Porch Swing

This fun and easy quilt has fusible appliqué and a stunning prairie-point border finish, and it can be made with 5" charms.

Designed & Quilted by Nancy Walhout Recker

Skill Level

Confident Beginner

Finished Size

Quilt Size: 50" x 62" (excluding prairie points)
Block Size: 6" x 6"
Number of Blocks: 80

Materials

- 168 assorted 5" precut squares
- 3½ yards white-with-green print
- Backing to size
- Batting to size
- Thread
- Template material
- 3 yards fusible web with paper release
- Basic sewing tools and supplies

Project Notes

Read all instructions before beginning this project.

Stitch right sides together using a ¼" seam allowance unless otherwise specified.

Materials and cutting lists assume 40" of usable fabric width for yardage.

Cutting

From white-with-green print:

- Cut 6 (1¼" by fabric width) binding strips.
- Cut 14 (6½" by fabric width) strips.
  Subcut strips into 80 (6½") A squares.
- Cut 6 (1½" by fabric width) C/D strips.

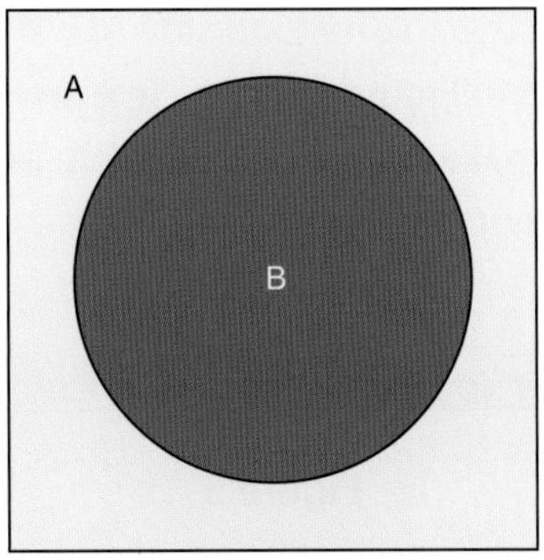

Porch Swing
6" x 6" Finished Block
Make 80

Completing the Blocks

1. Referring to Raw-Edge Fusible Appliqué on page 10, prepare B circle template using pattern provided on page 9. Use template to trace 80 B circles on paper side of fusible web and cut out.

2. Fuse B circles to wrong side of precut squares. Cut out and remove backing paper.

3. Center B circle on an A square as shown in Figure 1 and fuse in place according to manufacturer's directions. Repeat to make a total of 80 blocks.

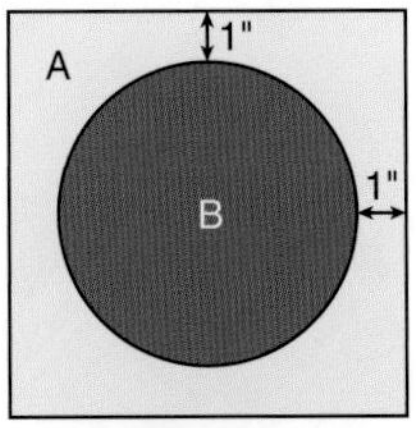

Figure 1

4. Using your chosen machine stitch, stitch B circles in place. Sample was stitched with a blanket stitch.

Prairie Points

Easy to make, prairie points are a fun addition to quilt edges or even as insertions in blocks or borders to give your quilt depth and movement with a sawtooth detail.

1. Fold a square in half diagonally (Figure A) and press.

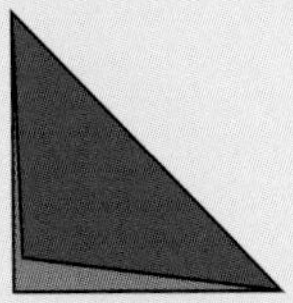

Figure A

2. Fold in half again and press referring to Figure B.

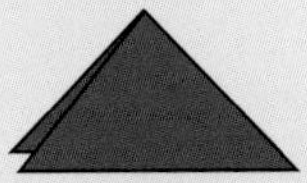

Figure B

3. To add prairie points to a seam, pin the first point to the seam edge and then tuck the consecutive prairie point ends between the folds of the previous prairie points and pinning in place (Figure C). Baste the prairie points in place.

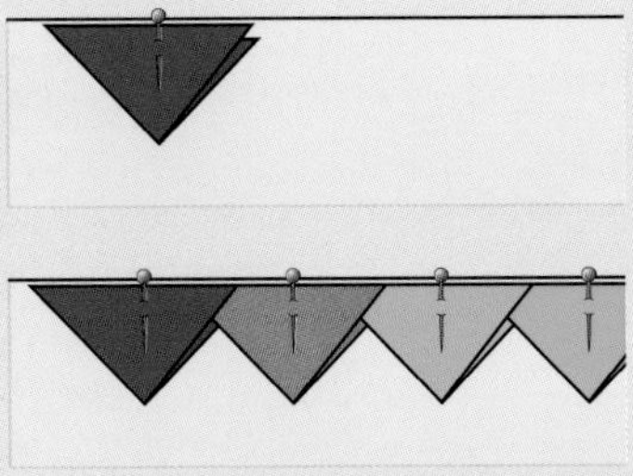

Figure C

To use prairie points as a binding embellishment on quilted projects:

4. After quilting and trimming the quilt top, batting and backing even, add prairie points around the quilt edges referring to step 3, with prairie points pointed toward the quilt center. Baste to hold in place. ***Note:*** *Adjust how far the points are inserted together for even spacing.* Finish quilt with binding.

Completing the Quilt

Refer to the Assembly Diagram for positioning of blocks and borders.

1. Arrange blocks in 10 rows of eight blocks each. Stitch blocks into rows; press. Stitch rows together to complete quilt center; press.

2. Sew C/D strips together on short ends to make one long strip. Cut two each 1½" x 60½" C strips and 1½" x 50½" D strips.

3. Sew C strips to opposite long sides of pieced center; press. Sew D strips to top and bottom to complete the quilt top; press.

4. Layer and quilt as desired. Trim backing and batting even with quilt top.

5. Referring to Prairie Points tutorial at left, make 88 prairie points using remaining precut squares.

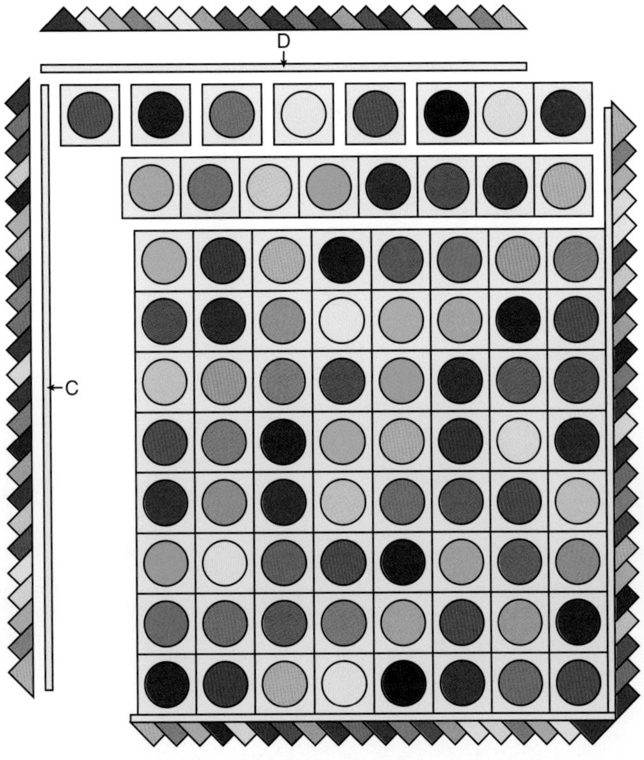

Porch Swing
Assembly Diagram 50" x 62" excluding prairie points

6. Arrange 24 prairie points on each side of quilt and 20 prairie points each along top and bottom, beginning and ending ½" from each corner; baste in place.

7. Stitch binding strips on short ends to make one long strip; press. Cut two each 1¼" x 52" and 1¼" x 64" binding strips.

8. With right sides together and raw edges matching, center and stitch the longer strips to the sides of the quilt, being careful not to catch the top and bottom prairie points in the stitching.

9. Turn binding to the back, pulling prairie points to the outside. Turn the long edge of binding under ¼" and hand-stitch in place. Trim strip ends even with the quilt at the top and bottom.

10. Repeat steps 8 and 9 with the shorter strips on the top and bottom, except trim each end of the strips ½" beyond the side edges of the quilt. Fold the ½" inside the binding before stitching in place to complete the quilt. ●

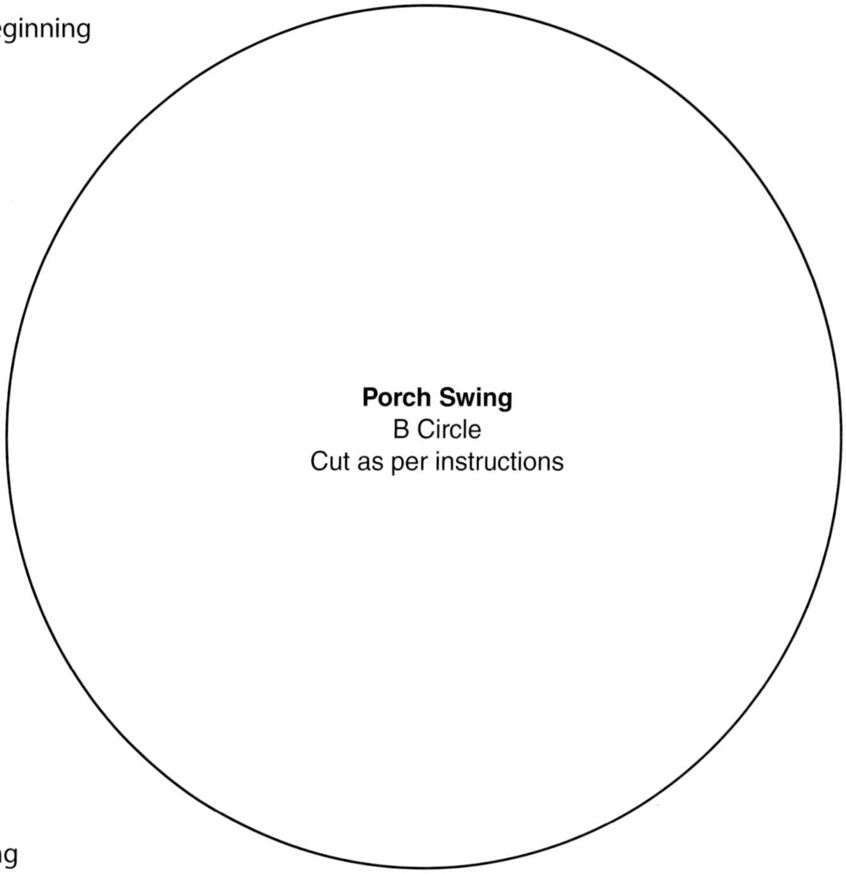

Raw-Edge Fusible Appliqué

One of the easiest ways to appliqué is the raw-edge fusible-web method. Paper-backed fusible web individual pieces are fused to the wrong side of specified fabrics, cut out and then fused together in a motif or individually to a foundation fabric, where they are machine-stitched in place.

Choosing Appliqué Fabrics

Depending on the appliqué, you may want to consider using batiks. Batik is a much tighter weave and, because of the manufacturing process, does not fray. If you are thinking about using regular quilting cottons, be sure to stitch your raw-edge appliqués with blanket/buttonhole stitches instead of a straight stitch.

Cutting Appliqué Pieces

1. Fusible appliqué shapes should be reversed for this technique.

2. Trace the appliqué shapes onto the paper side of paper-backed fusible web. Leave at least ¼" between shapes. Cut out shapes leaving a margin around traced lines. ***Note:*** *If doing several identical appliqués, trace reversed shapes onto template material to make reusable templates for tracing shapes onto the fusible web.*

3. Follow manufacturer's instructions and fuse shapes to wrong side of fabric as indicated on pattern for color and number to cut.

4. Cut out appliqué shapes on traced lines. Remove paper backing from shapes.

5. Again following fusible web manufacturer's instructions, arrange and fuse pieces to quilt referring to quilt pattern. Or fuse together shapes on top of an appliqué ironing mat to make an appliqué motif that can then be fused to the quilt.

Stitching Appliqué Edges

Machine-stitch appliqué edges to secure the appliqués in place and help finish the raw edges with matching or invisible thread (Photo 1). ***Note:*** *To show stitching, all samples have been stitched with contrasting thread.*

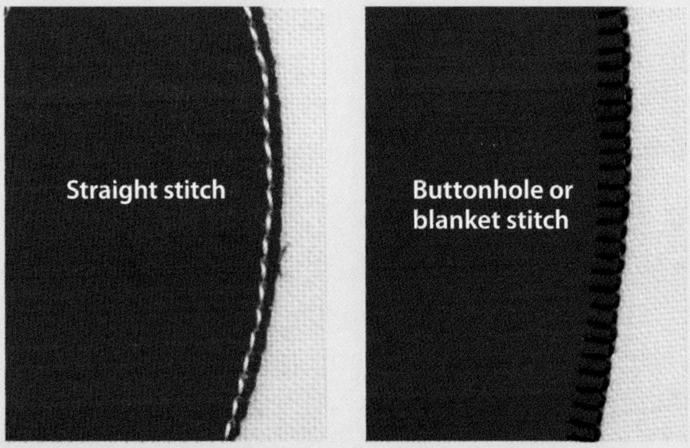

Photo 1

Invisible thread can be used to stitch appliqués down when using the blanket or straight stitches. Do not use it for the satin stitch. Definitely practice with invisible thread before using it on your quilt; it can sometimes be difficult to work with.

A short, narrow buttonhole or blanket stitch is most commonly used (Photo 2). Your machine manual may also refer to this as an appliqué stitch. Be sure to stitch next to the appliqué edge with the stitch catching the appliqué.

Photo 2

Practice turning inside and outside corners on scrap fabric before stitching appliqué pieces. Learn how your machine stitches so that you can make the pivot points smooth.

1. To stitch outer corners, stitch to the edge of the corner and stop with needle in the fabric at the corner point. Pivot to the next side of the corner and continue to sew (Photo 3). You will get a box on an outside corner.

Photo 3

2. To stitch inner corners, pivot at the inner point with needle in fabric (Photo 4). You will see a Y shape in the corner.

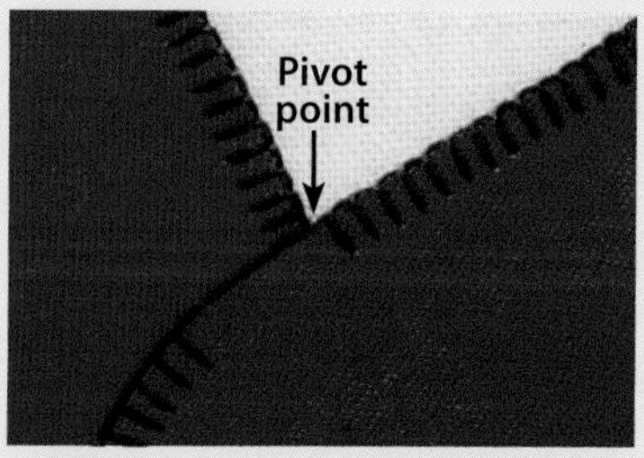

Photo 4

3. You can also use a machine straight stitch. Turn corners in the same manner, stitching to the corners and pivoting with needle in down position (Photo 5).

Photo 5

General Appliqué Tips

1. Use a light- to medium-weight stabilizer behind an appliqué to keep the fabric from puckering during machine stitching (Photo 6).

Photo 6

2. To reduce the stiffness of a finished appliqué, cut out the center of the fusible web shape, leaving ¼"–½" inside the pattern line. This gives a border of adhesive to fuse to the background and leaves the center soft and easy to quilt.

3. If an appliqué fabric is so light colored or thin that the background fabric shows through, fuse a lightweight interfacing to the wrong side of the fabric. You can also fuse a piece of the appliqué fabric to a matching piece, wrong sides together, and then apply the fusible with a drawn pattern to one side.

Dancing in the Rain

This is the perfect pattern to showcase a collection of charm squares.

Designed & Quilted by Bev Getschel

Skill Level
Confident Beginner

Finished Size
Quilt Size: 48" x 52"

Block Size: 4" x 4"

Number of Blocks: 78

Materials
- 39 assorted 5" precut squares
- ⅝ yard red solid
- 2⅓ yards white tonal
- Backing to size
- Batting to size
- Thread
- Basic sewing tools and supplies

Project Notes
Read all instructions before beginning this project.

Stitch right sides together using a ¼" seam allowance unless otherwise specified.

Materials and cutting lists assume 40" of usable fabric width for yardage.

Cutting

From precut squares:
- Cut 156 (2½") A squares.

From red solid:
- Cut 6 (2½" by fabric width) binding strips.

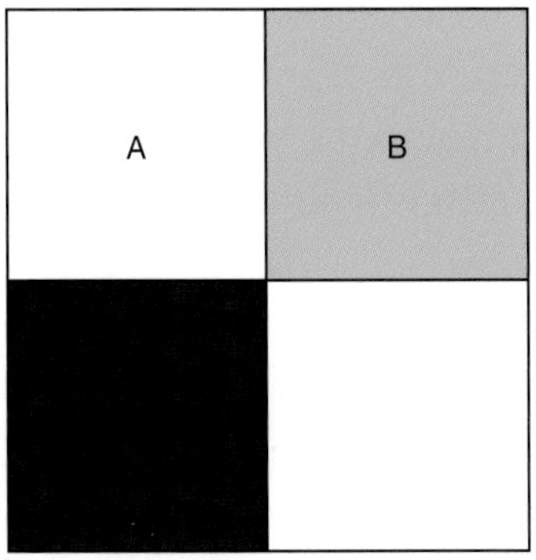

Four-Patch
4" x 4" Finished Block
Make 78

From white tonal:
- Cut 10 (2½" by fabric width) strips.
  Subcut strips into 156 (2½") B squares.
- Cut 10 (4½" by fabric width) strips.
  Subcut strips into 78 (4½") C squares.

Completing the Blocks
1. Referring to Figure 1, sew two each A and B squares together to make two rows; press. Sew rows together to make a Four-Patch block; press. Repeat to make a total of 78 Four-Patch blocks.

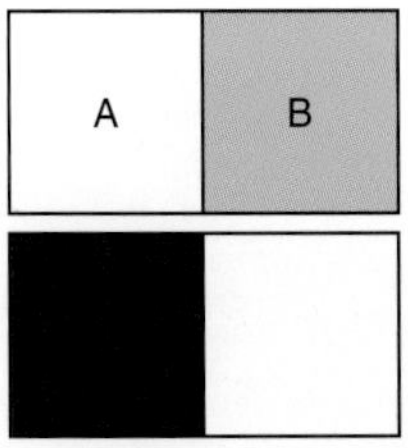

Figure 1

Westclox

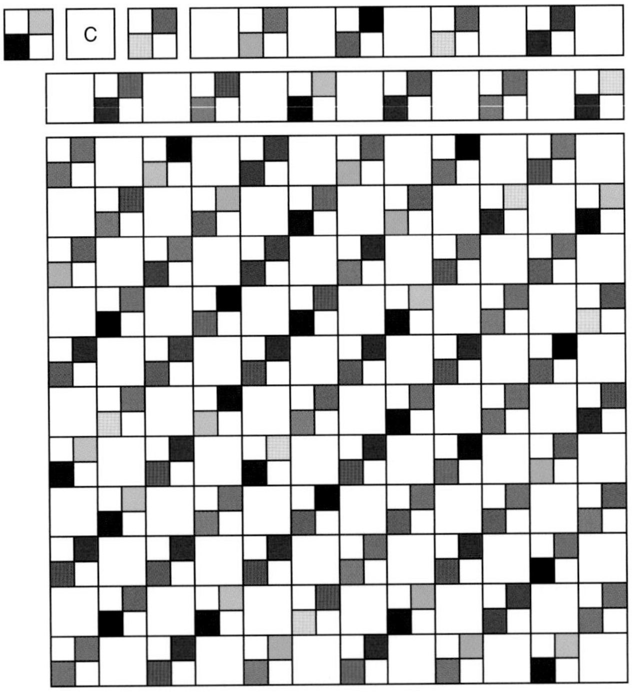

Dancing in the Rain
Assembly Diagram 48" x 52"

Completing the Quilt

Refer to the Assembly Diagram for positioning of blocks and squares.

1. Sew together six Four-Patch blocks alternately with six C squares to form a row; press. Repeat to make 13 rows.

2. Sew rows together to complete the quilt top, turning every other row to offset blocks and squares; press.

3. Layer, quilt and bind referring to Quilting Basics on page 45. ●

Festival Quilt

Here's a pattern that is simple yet will show off those 5" morsels of gorgeous fabrics. This one could be completed in a day.

Design by Lyn Brown
Quilted by Cathy O'Brien

Skill Level
Beginner

Finished Size
Quilt Size: 50" x 72"

Materials
- 43 assorted 5" precut batik squares
- ⅝ yard peach batik
- 2⅛ yards white tonal
- Backing to size
- Batting to size
- Thread
- Basic sewing tools and supplies

Project Notes
Read all instructions before beginning this project.

Stitch right sides together using a ¼" seam allowance unless otherwise specified.

Materials and cutting lists assume 41" of usable fabric width for yardage.

Here's a Tip
Watch for directional fabrics and think about how you want to cut them. For this quilt, the pieces were cut going with the lines of the fabric since the overall design of the quilt is vertical.

Cutting

From precut squares:
- Select 39 squares and cut 78 (2½" x 5") A rectangles.
- Select 4 squares and cut 4 (2½" x 2¾") B rectangles.

From peach batik:
- Cut 7 (2½" by fabric width) binding strips.

From white tonal:
- Cut 1 (72½" by fabric width) strip.
  Subcut strip into 1 (13½" x 72½") C rectangle and 1 (27½" x 72½") D rectangle.

Completing the Quilt

Refer to the Assembly Diagram for positioning of pieces and strips.

1. Sew 16 A rectangles together on short ends to make one A row as shown in Figure 1; press. Repeat to make a total of three A rows.

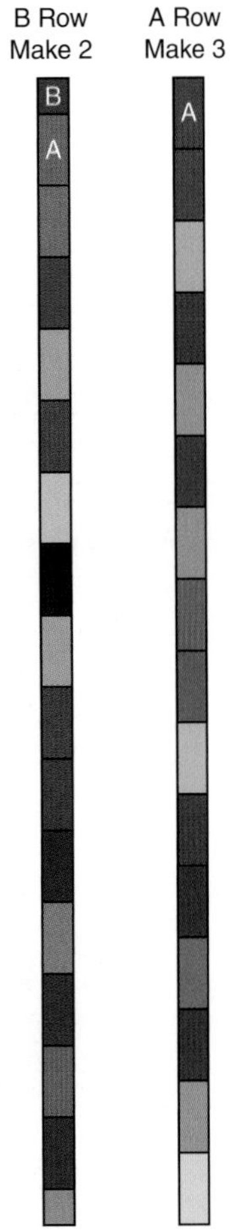

Figure 1

2. Again referring to Figure 1, sew 15 A and two B rectangles together on short ends to make one B row; press. Repeat to make a total of two B rows.

3. Alternately sew A and B rows together on the long sides to make a pieced center unit, press.

4. Stitch C and D rectangles to opposite sides of pieced center unit to complete the quilt top; press.

5. Layer, quilt and bind referring to Quilting Basics on page 45. ●

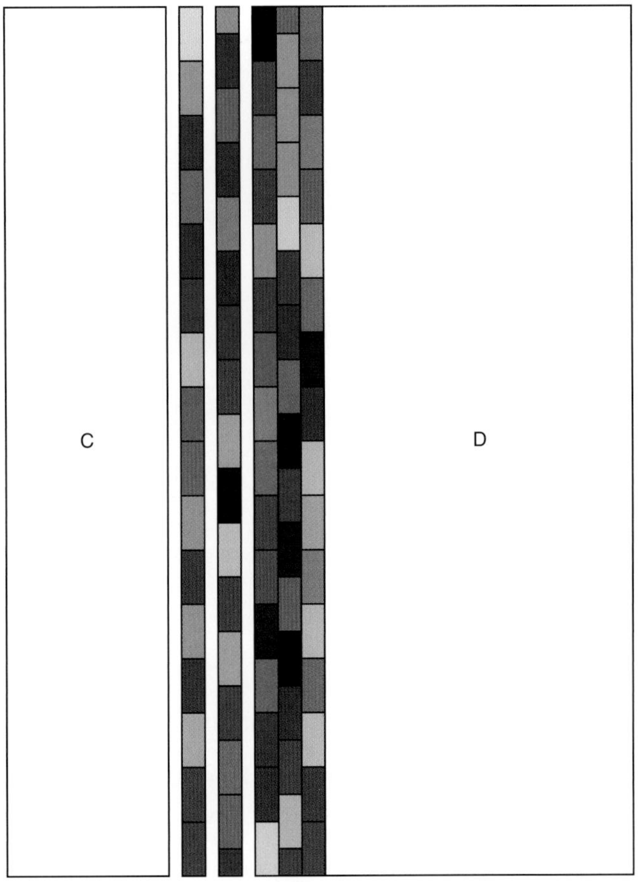

Festival Quilt
Assembly Diagram 50" x 72"

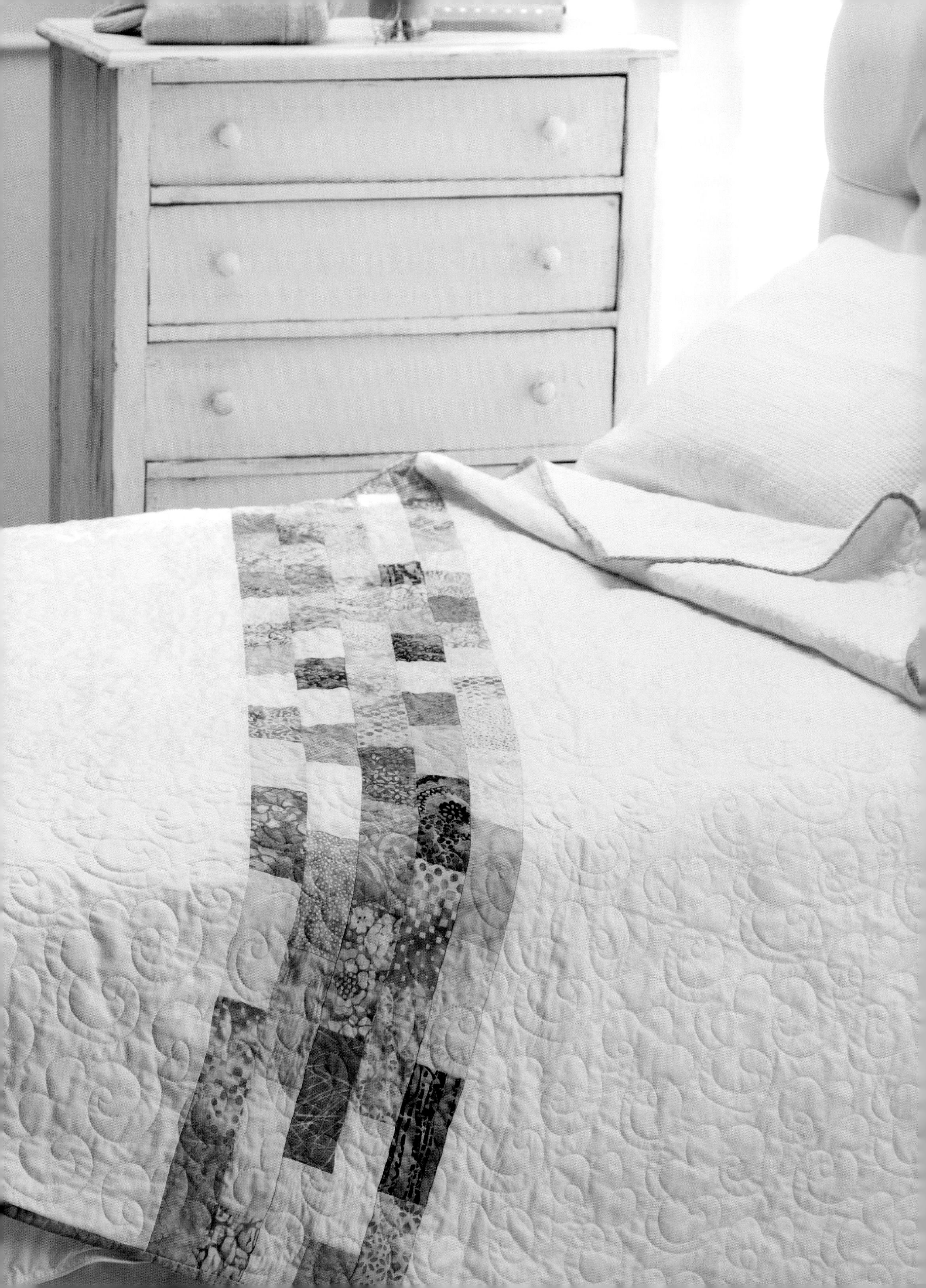

Charming Stars & Pinwheels

Make a romantic quilt with a soft background and the use of charm squares. Take the mystery out of fabric selection when you use packaged sets of precut 5" squares.

Design by Nancy Scott
Quilted by Masterpiece Quilting

Skill Level

Confident Beginner

Finished Size

Quilt Size: 90½" x 90½"
Block Size: 16" x 16"
Number of Blocks: 25

Materials

- 132 assorted 5" precut squares for A
- 6¾ yards light peach solid
- Backing to size
- Batting to size
- Thread
- Basic sewing tools and supplies

Project Notes

Read all instructions before beginning this project.

Stitch right sides together using a ¼" seam allowance unless otherwise specified.

Materials and cutting lists assume 40" of usable fabric width for yardage.

Cutting

From light peach solid:

- Cut 10 (2½" by fabric width) binding strips.

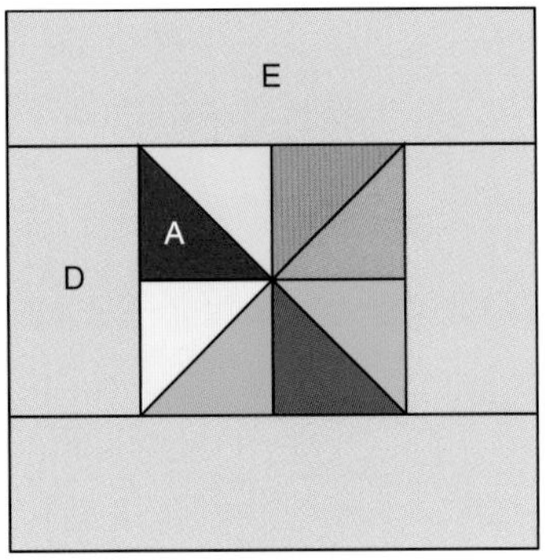

Pinwheel
16" x 16" Finished Block
Make 9

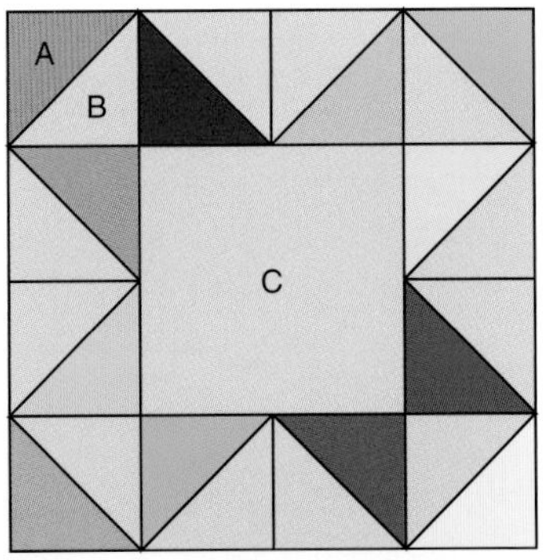

Star
16" x 16" Finished Block
Make 16

Here's a Tip

Since precut edges are pinked and die-cut, be sure to take the time to trim the half-square triangle units to 4½" square. It will ensure greater success when you are piecing the blocks.

- Cut 3 (23⅞" by fabric width) strips.
  Subcut strips into 3 (23⅞") squares. Cut each square on both diagonals to make 12 F triangles.
  Subcut remainder of strips into 6 (8½" by remaining fabric width) D strips and 3 (5" by remaining fabric width) B strips. Subcut strips into 18 (4½" x 8½") D rectangles and 9 (5") B squares.
- Cut 1 (12¼" by fabric width) strip.
  Subcut strip into 2 (12¼") G squares and 4 (5") B squares. Cut each G square in half on 1 diagonal to make 4 G triangles.
- Cut 4 (8½" by fabric width) strips.
  Subcut strips into 16 (8½") C squares and 4 (5") B squares.
- Cut 3 (16½" by fabric width) strips.
  Subcut strips into 18 (4½" x 16½") E rectangles and 18 (5") B squares.
- Cut 8 (5" by fabric width) strips.
  Subcut strips into 61 (5") squares to total 96 B squares.

Completing the Blocks

1. Draw a diagonal line from corner to corner on the wrong side of 114 A squares.

2. With right sides together, pair a marked A square with a B square. Stitch ¼" on each side of drawn line as shown in Figure 1. Cut on drawn line and press to yield two A-B units. Trim each unit to 4½" square, keeping seam centered. Repeat to make a total of 192 A-B units.

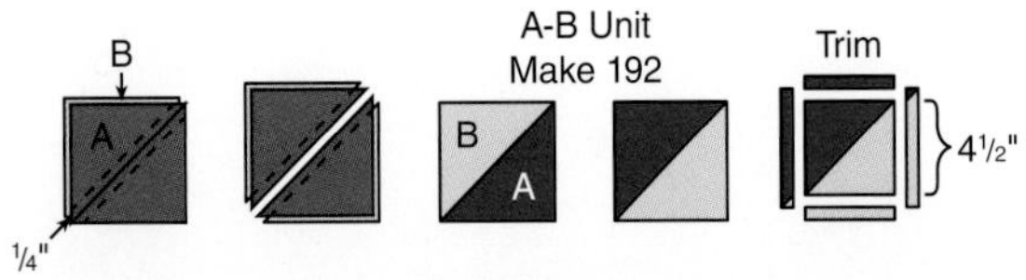

Figure 1

3. Referring to Figure 2, sew two A-B units together to make a side unit; press. Repeat to make a total of 32 side units.

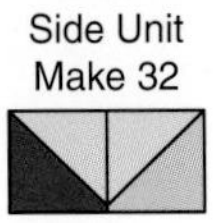

Figure 2

4. Arrange and sew four A-B units together as shown in Figure 3 to make a top/bottom unit; press. Repeat to make a total of 32 top/bottom units.

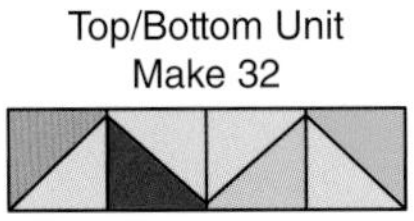

Figure 3

5. Referring to Figure 4, sew side units to opposite sides of a C square and top/bottom units to long sides of the pieced unit to complete one Star block; press. Repeat to make a total of 16 Star blocks.

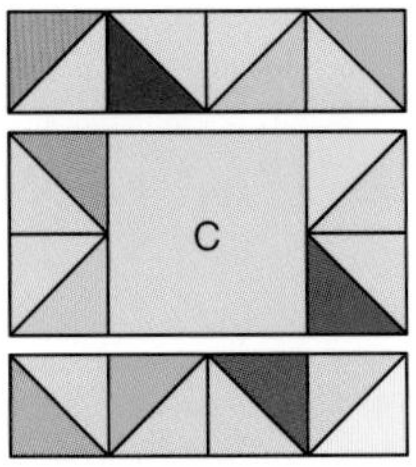

Figure 4

6. With right sides together, pair a marked A square and an unmarked A square and stitch ¼" on each side of drawn line as shown in Figure 5. Cut on drawn line and press to yield two A-A units. Trim each unit to 4½" square, keeping seam centered. Repeat to make a total of 36 A-A units.

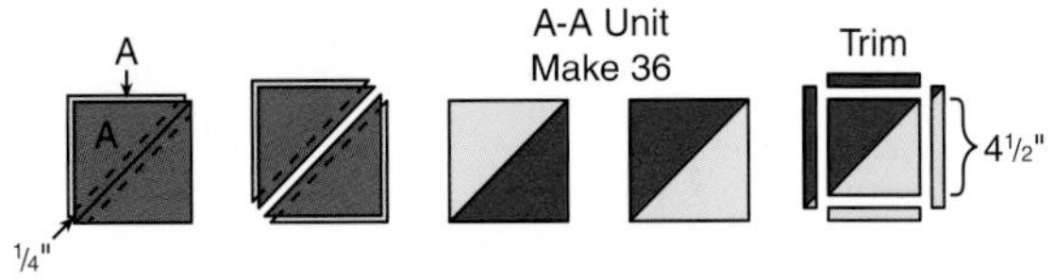

Figure 5

7. Referring to Figure 6, sew two A-A units together to make a row; press. Repeat to make a total of 18 rows.

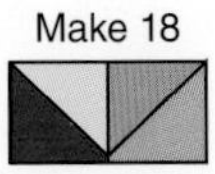

Figure 6

Figure 7

8. Arrange and stitch two rows together to form a pinwheel center as shown in Figure 7; press. Repeat to make a total of nine pinwheel centers.

9. Referring to Figure 8, sew D rectangles to opposite sides of the pinwheel center and E rectangles to the top and bottom to complete one Pinwheel block; press. Repeat to make a total of nine Pinwheel blocks.

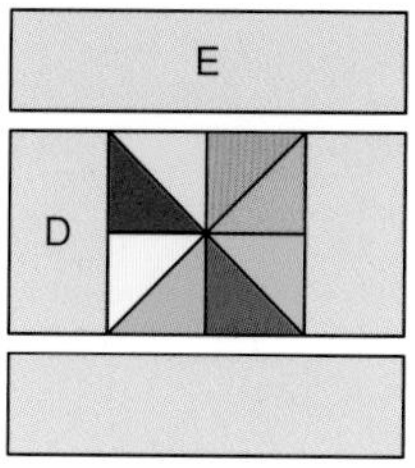

Figure 8

Completing the Quilt

Refer to the Assembly Diagram for positioning of blocks and triangles.

1. Arrange and stitch Star blocks, Pinwheel blocks and F and G triangles into diagonal rows; press.

2. Sew diagonal rows together and add a G triangle to opposite corners to complete the quilt top; press.

3. Layer, quilt and bind referring to Quilting Basics on page 45. ●

Charming Stars & Pinwheels
Assembly Diagram 90½" x 90½"

Crossing Lines

Discover just how versatile precut squares can be. Turn a charm pack and some coordinating fabric into a fabulous table runner with the help of some easy paper piecing.

Designed & Quilted by Connie Kauffman

Skill Level

Confident Beginner

Finished Size

Table Runner Size: 37½" x 15"

Materials

- 40 assorted 5" precut batik squares
- ⅝ yard light green batik
- Backing to size
- Batting to size
- Thread
- Paper-piecing paper
- Basic sewing tools and supplies

Project Notes

Read all instructions before beginning this project.

Stitch right sides together using a ¼" seam allowance unless otherwise specified.

Materials and cutting lists assume 40" of usable fabric width for yardage.

Cutting

From light green batik:

- Cut 4 (4" by fabric width) strips.
  Subcut strips into 40 (4") squares. Cut each square in half on 1 diagonal to make 80 triangles for sections 2 and 3.

Completing the Table Runner

Refer to the Assembly Diagram for positioning of units.

1. Print 40 copies of the paper-piecing pattern. Cut out each pattern, leaving a margin around the outside solid line.

2. Select four patterns. Referring to Figure 1, draw a line on each pattern ¼" into section 4. Trim on marked line to make patterns for four B units. Use 36 remaining patterns for A units.

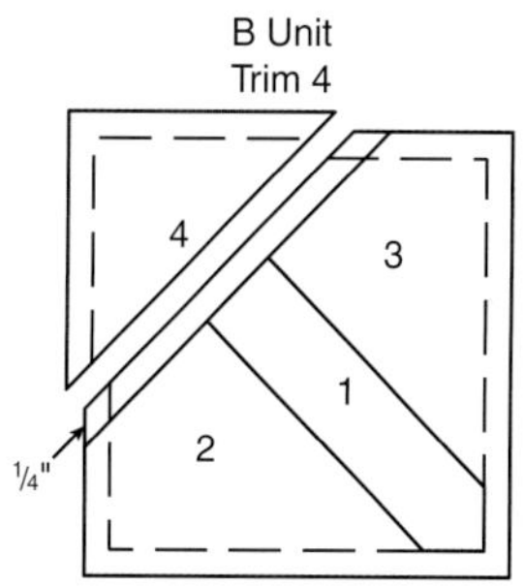

Figure 1

3. Referring to Paper Piecing tutorial on page 26 and Figures 2 and 3, paper-piece each A and B unit using one precut square for sections 1 and 4 and the previously cut triangles for sections 2 and 3.

Figure 2

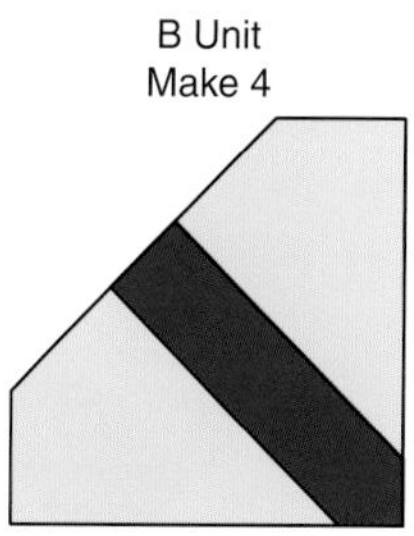

Figure 3

4. Trim fabric even with the outside solid line of each unit.

5. Arrange A and B units in four rows of 10 units each. Sew units into rows; press. Sew rows together to complete table runner top; press. Remove paper patterns.

6. Layer and pin the batting; the backing, right side up; and the runner top, right side down. Sew ¼" from the edge, leaving a 3" opening. Trim corners and turn the runner right side out. Turn seam allowance in at the opening and stitch closed. Press and quilt as desired. ●

Crossing Lines
Assembly Diagram 37½" x 15"

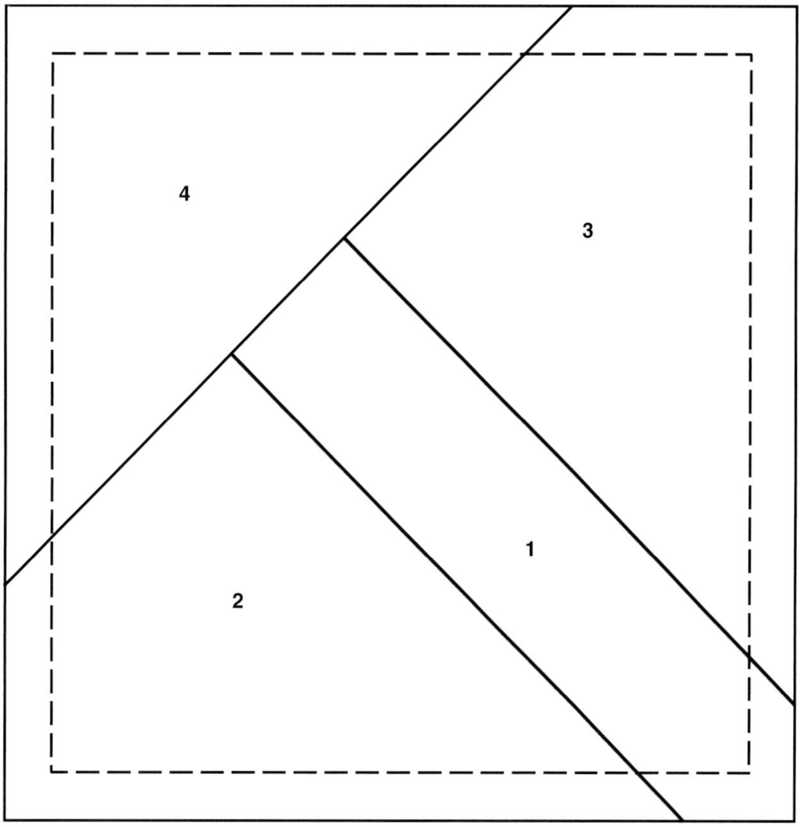

Crossing Lines
Paper-Piecing Pattern

Paper Piecing

Paper piecing allows a quilter to make blocks with odd-shaped and/or small pieces and more precise corners. Fabric pieces are sewn together onto the reverse side of a paper-piecing pattern, and then the paper is carefully removed when the block is completed. You may have to rethink how you piece when using this technique and it does require a little more yardage.

1. Make same-size copies of the paper-piecing pattern as directed in the pattern. There are several choices in transparent papers as well as water-soluble papers that can be used, which are available at your local office supply store, quilt shop or online. Some papers can be used in your printer.

2. Cut out the patterns leaving a margin around the outside bold lines as shown in Figure A. All patterns are reversed on the paper copies. Pattern color choices can be written in each numbered space on the marked side of each copy.

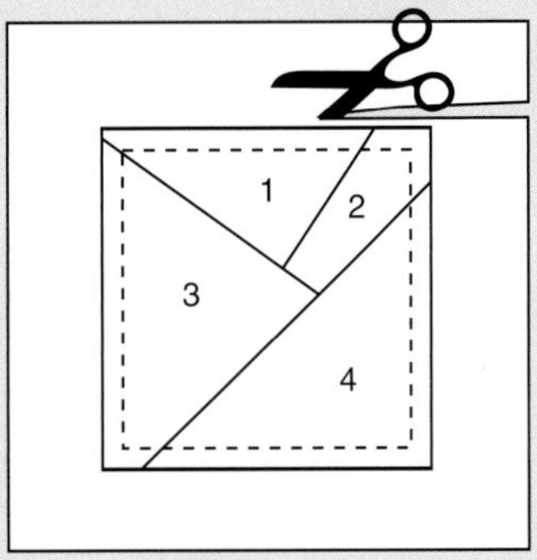

Figure A

3. When cutting fabric for paper piecing, the pieces do not have to be the exact size and shape of the area to be covered. Cut fabric pieces the general shape and ¼"–½" larger than the design area to be covered. This makes paper piecing a good way to use up scraps.

4. With the printed side of the pattern facing you, fold along each line of the pattern as shown in Figure B, creasing the stitching lines. This will help in trimming the fabric seam allowances and in removing the paper when you are finished stitching. ***Note:*** *You can also machine stitch along the lines with a basting stitching and no thread to perforate the paper.*

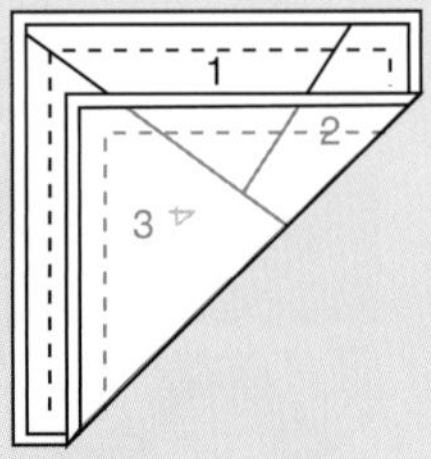

Figure B

5. Turn the paper pattern over with the unmarked side facing you and position fabric indicated on pattern right side up over the space marked 1. Hold the paper up to a window or over a light box to make sure that the fabric overlaps all sides of space 1 at least ¼" as shown in Figure C from the printed side of the pattern. Pin to hold fabric in place. ***Note:*** *You can also use a light touch of glue stick. Too much glue will make the paper difficult to remove.*

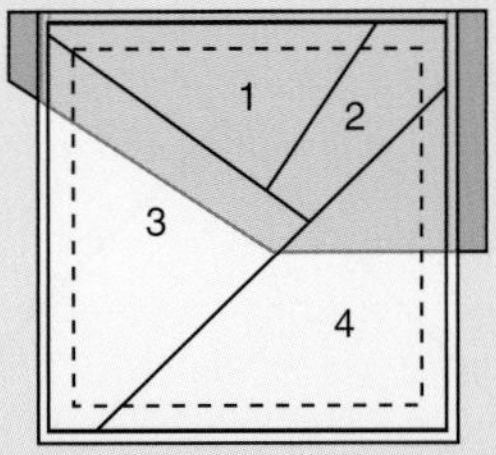

Figure C

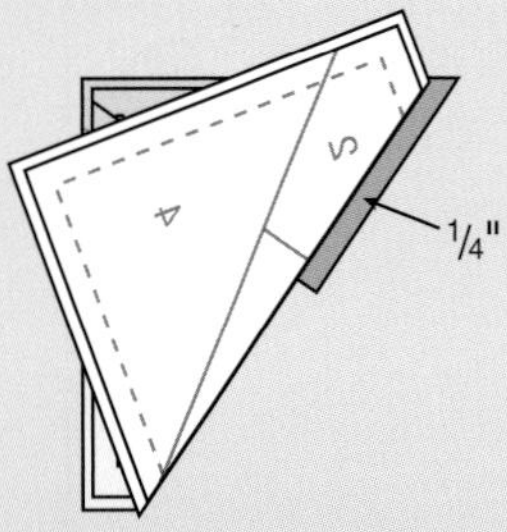

Figure D

6. Turn the paper over with the right side of the paper facing you, and fold the paper along the lines between sections 1 and 2. Trim fabric to about ¼" from the folded edge as shown in Figure D.

7. Place the second fabric indicated right sides together with first piece. Fabric edges should be even along line between spaces 1 and 2 as shown in Figure E. Fold fabric over and check to see if second fabric piece will cover space 2.

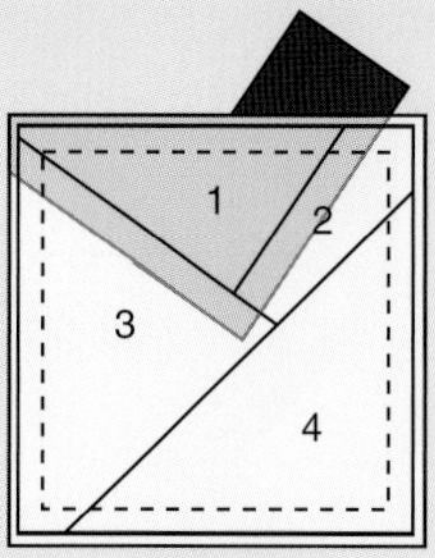

Figure E

8. With the right side of the paper facing you, hold fabric pieces together and stitch along the line between spaces 1 and 2 as shown in Figure F using a very small stitch length (18–20 stitches per inch). ***Note:*** *Using a smaller stitch length will make removing paper easier because it creates a tear line at the seam. Always begin and end seam by sewing two to three stitches beyond the line. You do not need to backstitch. Start sewing at the solid outside line of the pattern when the beginning of the seam is at the edge of the pattern.*

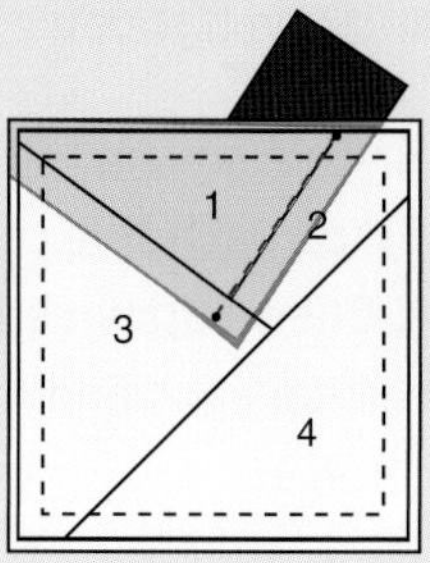

Figure F

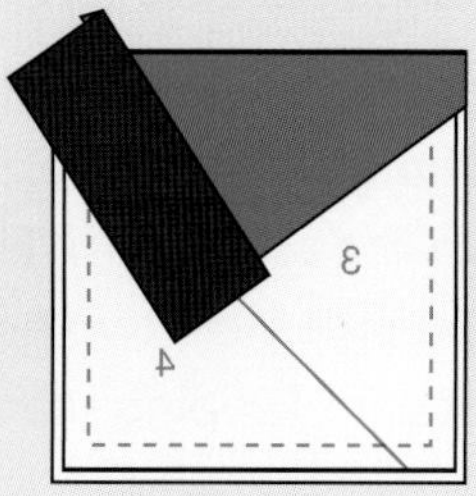

Figure G

9. Turn the pattern over, flip the second fabric back and finger-press as shown in Figure G.

10. Continue trimming and sewing pieces in numerical order until the pattern is completely covered. Make sure pieces along the outer edge extend past the solid line to allow for a ¼" seam allowance as shown in Figure H.

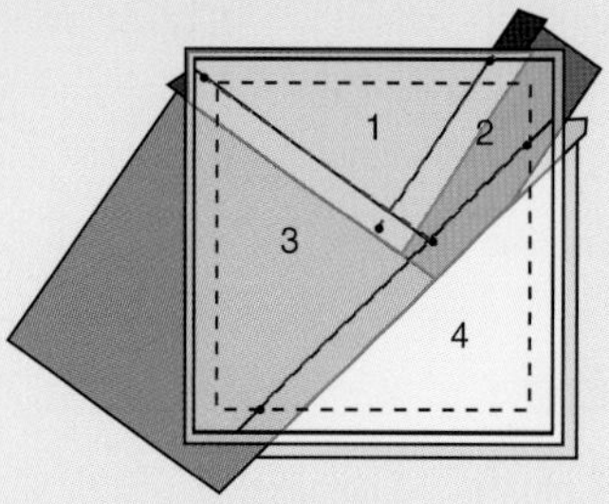

Figure H

11. When the whole block is sewn, press the block and trim all excess fabric from the block along the outside-edge solid line of paper pattern as shown in Figure I.

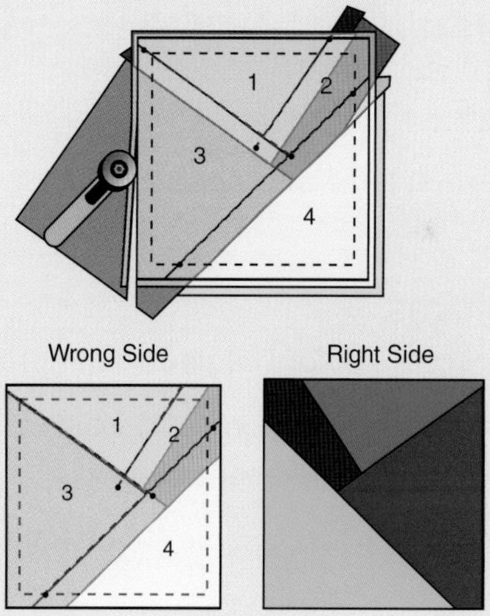

Figure I

12. After stitching blocks together, carefully remove the backing paper from completed blocks and press seams. You can also staystitch ⅛" from the outer edge of the completed block. Carefully remove backing paper and press seams. Then complete quilt top assembly.

Charming Stars

Make these star blocks using 5" squares and half-square triangles. It couldn't be easier.

Design by Sharon Tucker
Quilted by Grass Roots Quilting

Skill Level

Confident Beginner

Finished Size

Runner Size: 80" x 16"

Block Size: 16" x 16"

Number of Blocks: 5

Materials

- 20 pairs of matching 5" precut squares
- 1⅝ yards off-white solid
- Backing to size
- Batting to size
- Thread
- Basic sewing tools and supplies

Project Notes

Read all instructions before beginning this project.

Stitch right sides together using a ¼" seam allowance unless otherwise specified.

Materials and cutting lists assume 40" of usable fabric width for yardage.

Cutting

From off-white solid:

- Cut 6 (2½" by fabric width) binding strips.
- Cut 3 (5" by fabric width) strips.
  Subcut strips into 20 (5") A squares.
- Cut 3 (4½" by fabric width) strips.
  Subcut strips into 20 (4½") D squares.

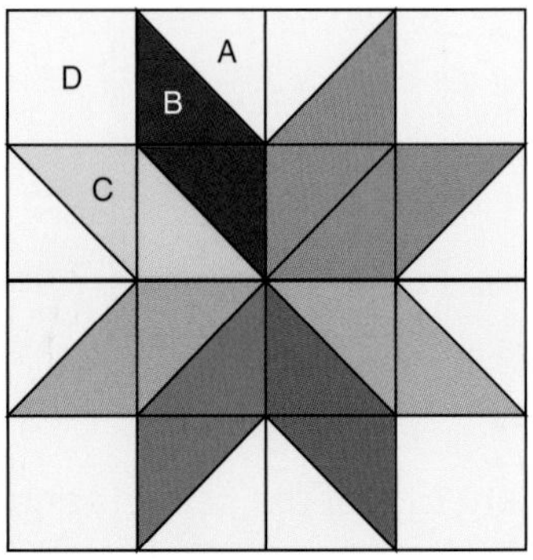

8-Point Star
16" x 16" Finished Block
Make 5

Completing the Blocks

1. To complete two quarter-blocks, select two each A and D squares. Select two different-color matching pairs of precut squares; label one pair B and one pair C.

2. Draw a diagonal line from corner to corner on the wrong side of both A squares and one B square.

3. With right sides together, pair an A square with the unmarked B square. Stitch ¼" on each side of drawn line as shown in Figure 1. Cut on drawn line and press to yield two A-B units. Trim each unit to 4½" square, keeping seam centered.

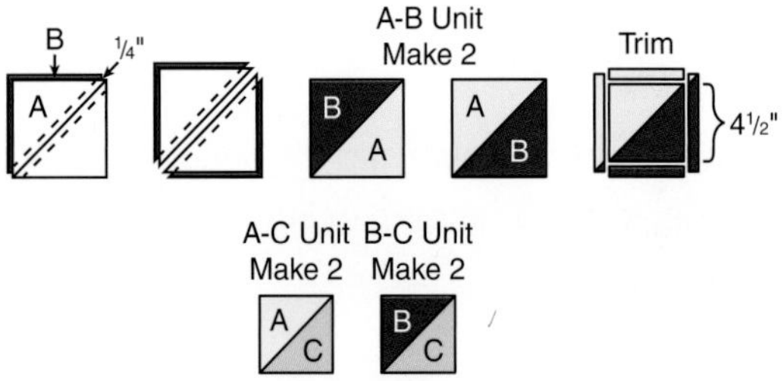

Figure 1

4. Repeat step 3 to make two each A-C units and B-C units.

5. Referring to Figure 2, arrange and sew an A-B unit and D square into one row and a B-C unit and A-C unit into a second row; press. Sew rows together to make a quarter-block. Repeat to make a second quarter-block.

Quarter-Block
Make 20

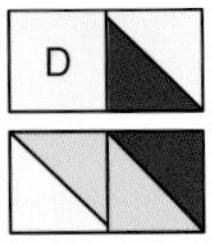

Figure 2

6. Repeat steps 1–5 to make a total of 20 quarter-blocks.

7. Select four different quarter-blocks. Referring to Figure 3, arrange and sew quarter-blocks into two rows; press. Sew rows together to complete one 8-Point Star block; press. Repeat to make a total of five 8-Point Star blocks.

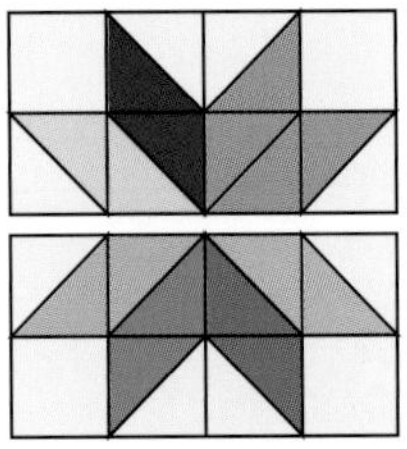

Figure 3

Completing the Runner

Refer to the Assembly Diagram for positioning of blocks.

1. Arrange and stitch 8-Point Star blocks into a long row to complete the top; press.

2. Layer, quilt and bind referring to Quilting Basics on page 45. ●

Here's a Tip

This basic 8-Point Star block can be used for more than a runner. Make a few more and create an easy throw quilt.

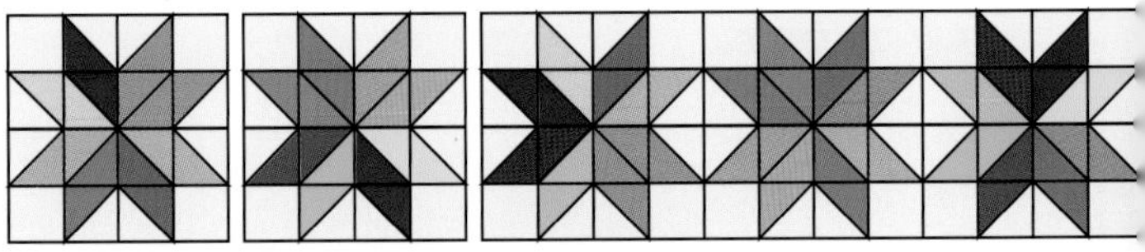

Charming Stars
Assembly Diagram 80" x 16"

Linear Quilt

Simple piecing using precut squares in striking colors makes this contemporary quilt a must for any quilter. All you need are precut squares and a coordinating fabric.

Design by Nancy Scott
Quilted by Masterpiece Quilting

Skill Level

Beginner

Finished Size

Quilt Size: 47½" x 55½"

Block Size: 4½" x 4½"

Number of Blocks: 63

Materials

- 99 assorted 5" precut squares
- 2 yards charcoal tonal
- Backing to size
- Batting to size
- Thread
- Basic sewing tools and supplies

Project Notes

Read all instructions before beginning this project.

Stitch right sides together using a ¼" seam allowance unless otherwise specified.

Materials and cutting lists assume 40" of usable fabric width for yardage.

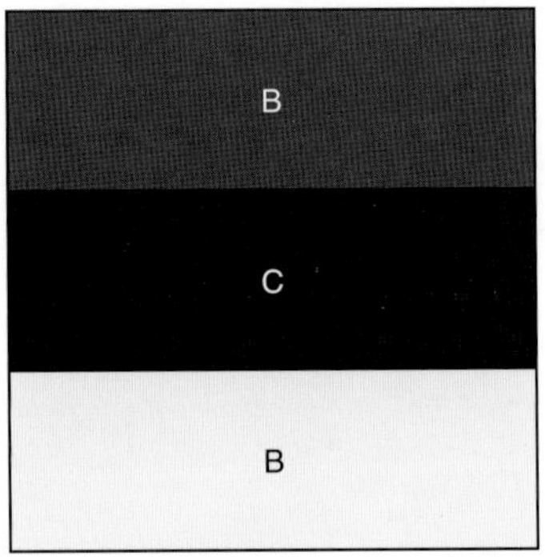

Linear
4½" x 4½" Finished Block
Make 63

Cutting

From precut squares:

- Select 36 squares and cut 72 (2½" x 5") A rectangles.
- Select 63 squares and cut 126 (2" x 5") B rectangles.

From charcoal tonal:

- Cut 6 (2½" by fabric width) binding strips.
- Cut 12 (2" by fabric width) D strips.
- Cut 4 (5" by fabric width) strips.
  Subcut strips into 63 (2" x 5") C rectangles.

Here's a Tip

Since precut-square edges are pinked, be sure to measure carefully from the outer edge of the "points" to get a true cut.

Completing the Blocks

1. Referring to Figure 1, sew a B rectangle to opposite long sides of a C rectangle to make a Linear block; press. Repeat to make a total of 63 Linear blocks.

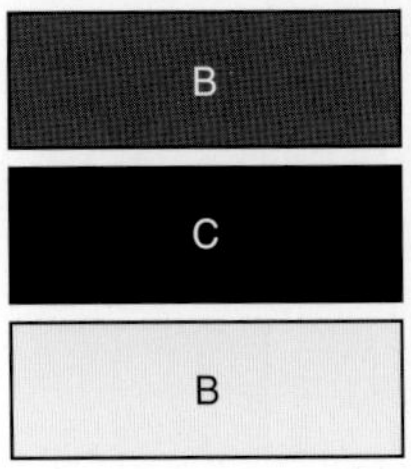

Figure 1

Blossoms of COLOR
EDGE

Completing the Quilt

Refer to the Assembly Diagram for positioning of blocks and strips.

1. Alternately sew eight A rectangles and seven Linear blocks together to make a pieced row, beginning and ending with an A rectangle; press. Repeat to make a total of nine pieced rows.

2. Sew D strips together on short ends to make one long strip; press. Subcut strip into 10 (2" x 48") D strips.

3. Alternately sew D strips and pieced rows together to complete the quilt top; press.

4. Layer, quilt and bind referring to Quilting Basics on page 45. ●

Linear Quilt
Assembly Diagram $47^{1/2}$" x $55^{1/2}$"

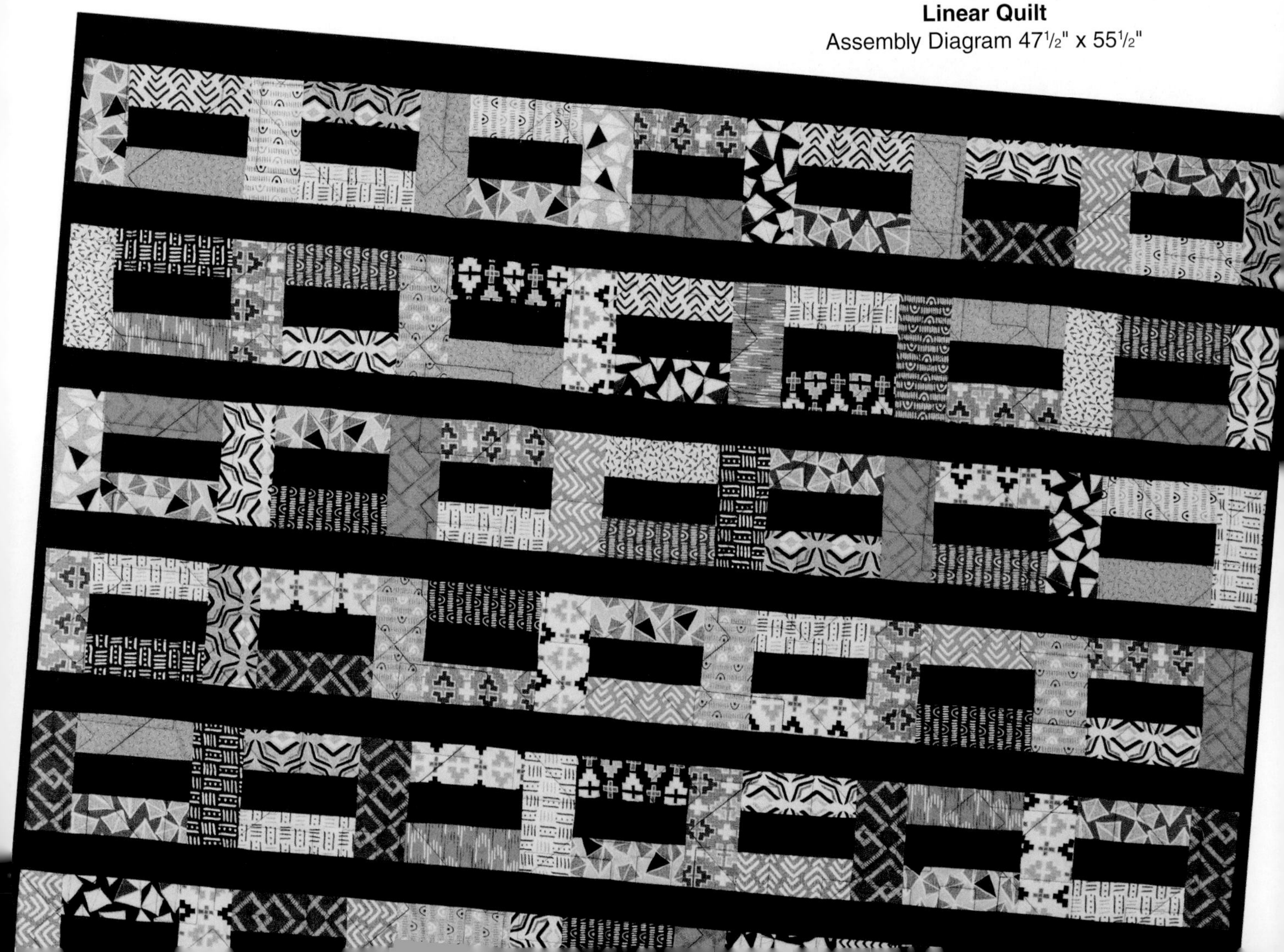

Butterfly Trio Hot Pads

Add a fun touch of color to your table with a set of colorful scrappy butterfly hot pads made in a day with leftover charms and a background fabric.

Designed & Quilted by Carolyn S. Vagts

Skill Level

Beginner

Finished Size

Hot Pad Size: 8½" x 8½" (including binding)

Block Size: 8" x 8" finished

Number of Blocks: 3

Materials

Fabrics listed are for 3 hot pads.

- 8 off-white 5" precut squares
- 3 assorted blue print 5" precut squares for C
- 1 each burgundy and teal 5" precut square
- ⅜ yard black solid
- Backing to size
- Cotton batting to size
- Insulated batting to size
- Thread
- Basic sewing tools and supplies

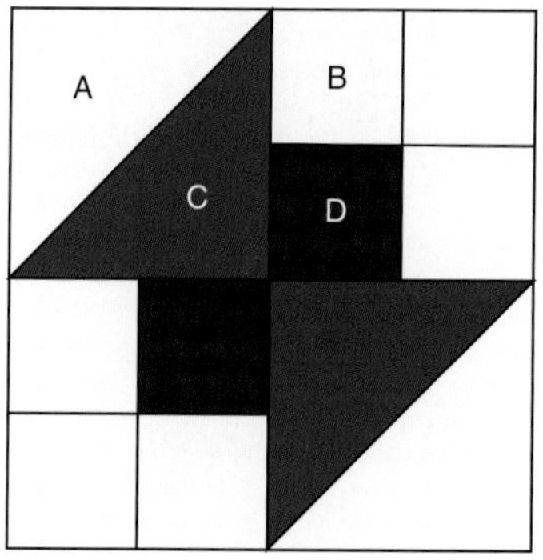

Butterfly
8" x 8" Finished Block
Make 3

Project Notes

Read all instructions before beginning this project.

Stitch right sides together using a ¼" seam allowance unless otherwise specified.

Materials and cutting lists assume 40" of usable fabric width for yardage.

Cutting

From off-white precut squares:

- Select 5 squares and cut 18 (2½") B squares.
- Label remaining squares A.

From burgundy precut square:

- Cut 4 (2½") D squares.

From teal precut square:

- Cut 2 (2½") D squares.

From black solid:

- Cut 4 (2¼" by fabric width) binding strips.

Completing the Hot Pads

1. Draw a diagonal line from corner to corner on the wrong side of each A square.

2. With right sides together, pair an A square with a C square. Stitch ¼" on each side of drawn line as shown in Figure 1. Cut on drawn line and press to yield two A-C units. Repeat to make a total of six A-C units.

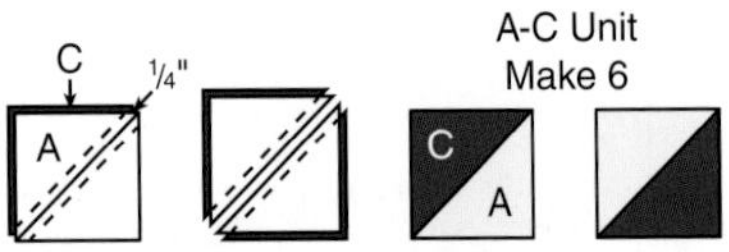

Figure 1

3. Sew two B squares together to form a row as shown in Figure 2; press. Repeat with one each B and D square. Sew rows together to form a B-D unit; press. Repeat to make six B-D units.

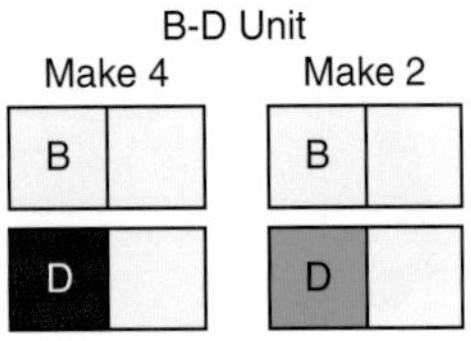

Figure 2

4. Referring to Figure 3, sew a B-D unit to an A-C unit to make a row; press. Repeat to make three matching pairs of rows.

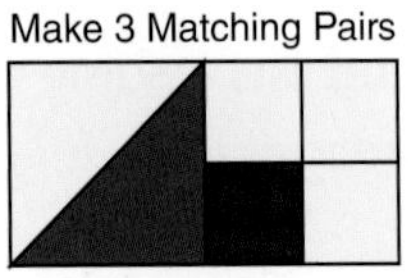

Figure 3

5. To complete a block, select one matching pair of rows and seam together referring to block diagram for orientation; press. Repeat to make a total of three blocks.

6. With a water-soluble marker and referring to the Placement Diagram, draw antenna lines, and wing and body loops on each block.

7. Layer the backing fabric, wrong side up; the insulated batting, shiny side down; cotton batting; and a block, right side up; pin-baste to hold. Repeat for each hot pad.

8. Quilt as desired. Use free-motion quilting with black thread to outline antennae and wing and body loops.

9. Bind referring to Quilting Basics on page 45. ●

Butterfly Trio Hot Pad
Placement Diagram 8½" x 8½" including binding

MASON

Sunset at the Beach

This is a fun and bright solution to a growing stash of 5" squares. You can purchase them to match or cut up scraps or use both. This could be an amazing stash buster.

Designed & Quilted by Nancy Walhout Recker

Skill Level

Confident Beginner

Finished Size

Quilt Size: 60" x 76"
Block Size: 16" x 16"
Number of Blocks: 12

Materials

- 32 assorted batik 5" precut squares
- 192 batik (5") precut squares in the following colors and quantities: 12 light green (A), 12 medium blue (B), 18 dark blue (C), 6 light yellow (D), 12 dark orange (E), 12 tan (F), 12 red (G), 12 dark green (H), 6 purple (I), 12 dark pink (J), 18 light pink (K), 18 red-violet (L), 6 teal (M), 12 turquoise (N), 12 dark yellow (O) and (12) medium orange (P)
- 1⅞ yards teal batik
- Backing to size
- Batting to size
- Thread
- Basic sewing tools and supplies

Project Notes

Read all instructions before beginning this project.

Stitch right sides together using a ¼" seam allowance unless otherwise specified.

Materials and cutting lists assume 40" of usable fabric width for yardage.

Sunset
16" x 16" Finished Block
Make 12

Cutting

From 32 assorted precut squares:

- Cut 64 (2½" x 4½") S rectangles.

From teal batik:

- Cut 7 (4½" by fabric width) Q/R strips.
- Cut 1 (2½" by fabric width) strip.
  Subcut strip into 4 (2½") T squares.
- Cut 8 (2¼" by fabric width) strips for binding.

Completing the Blocks

Refer to the block diagram for positioning of pieces.

1. Label the 192 precut squares with the letter given after each color in the Materials list.

2. Draw a diagonal line from corner to corner on the wrong side of six each A, D, F and N squares, and 12 each J and K squares.

3. With right sides together, pair a marked A square with a B square. Stitch ¼" on each side of drawn line as shown in Figure 1. Cut on drawn line and press to yield two A-B units. Trim each unit to 4½" square, keeping seam centered. Repeat to make a total of 12 A-B units.

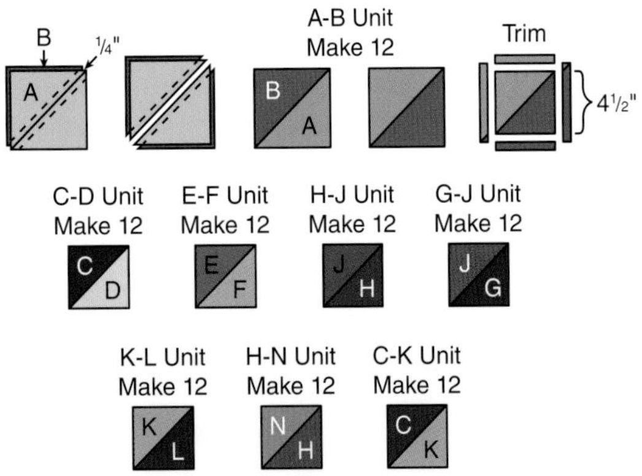

Figure 1

4. Repeat step 3 to make 12 each C-D, C-K, E-F, G-J, H-J, H-N and K-L units.

5. Draw a straight line in the center from top to bottom on the wrong side of each remaining F, I, K, L, M and O square.

6. With right sides together, pair an M square with a B square. Stitch ¼" on each side of drawn line as shown in Figure 2. Cut on drawn line and press to yield two B-M units. Trim each unit to 4½" square, keeping seam centered. Repeat to make a total of 12 B-M units.

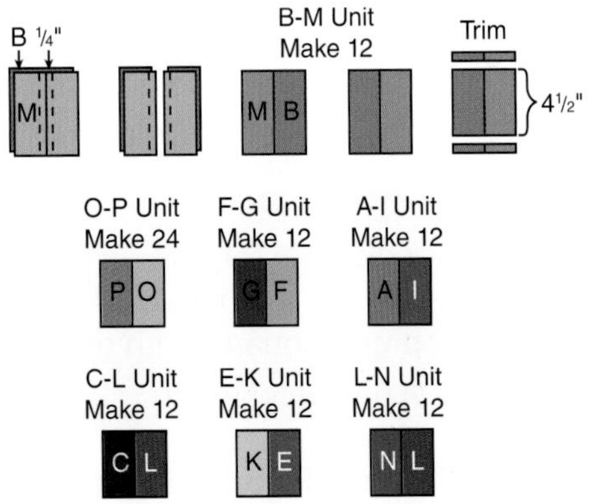

Figure 2

7. Repeat step 6 to make 12 each A-I, C-L, E-K, F-G and L-N units, and 24 O-P units.

8. Select one of each unit. Arrange units into four rows as shown in Figure 3. Stitch units into rows, press. Stitch rows together to complete one Sunset block; press. Repeat to make a total of 12 blocks.

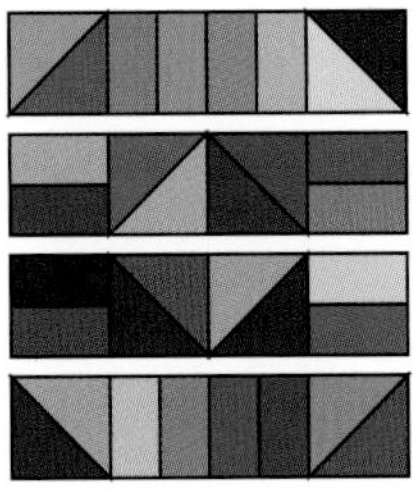

Figure 3

Completing the Quilt

Refer to the Assembly Diagram for positioning of blocks and strips.

1. Arrange Sunset blocks into four rows of three blocks each, rotating blocks as indicated in the Assembly Diagram. Stitch blocks into rows; press. Sew rows together to complete the pieced center; press.

2. Join Q/R strips on short ends to make one long strip; press. Subcut strip into two each 4½" x 64½" Q strips and 4½" x 56½" R strips.

3. Sew Q strips to opposite sides of pieced center; press. Sew R strips to top and bottom; press.

4. Referring to Figure 4, join 18 S rectangles on the short ends to make a long pieced border; press. Repeat to make a second long pieced border. Join 14 S rectangles and two T squares to make a short pieced border, press. Repeat to make a second short pieced border.

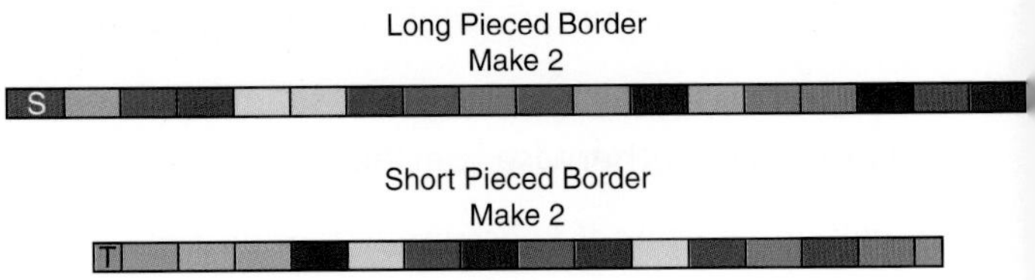

Figure 4

5. Sew long pieced borders to opposite sides and short pieced borders to top and bottom to complete the quilt top, press.

6. Layer, quilt and bind referring to Quilting Basics on page 45. ●

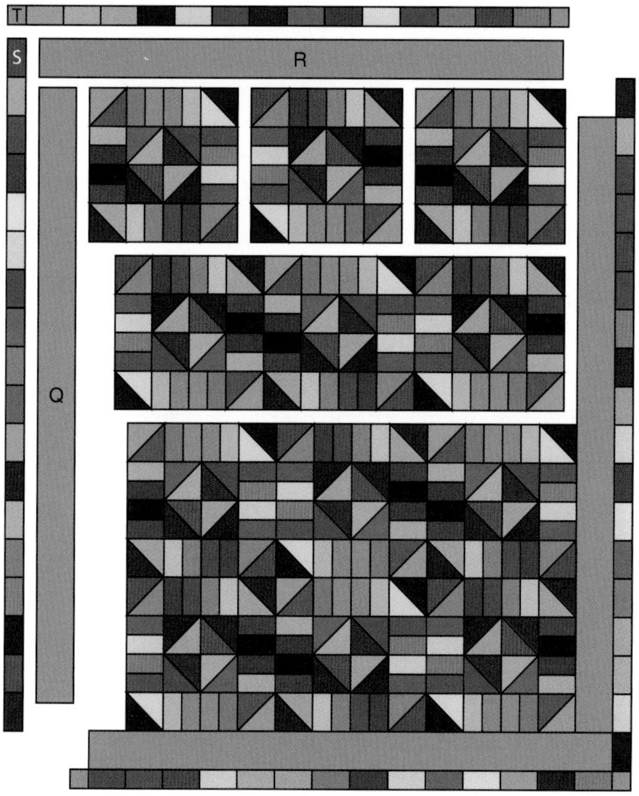

Sunset at the Beach
Assembly Diagram 60" x 76"

Refreshing Mug Rugs

Personalize a mug rug for that special friend who loves her or his coffee with creative quilted words. This is a great way to use your leftover 5" squares and make them count.

Designed & Quilted by Carolyn S. Vagts

Skill Level

Beginner

Finished Size

Mug Rug Size: 8½" x 10" (including binding)

Materials

Fabrics listed are for 1 mug rug.

- 1 each black and brown 5" precut square
- Fat quarter green or tan tonal
- ¼ yard black solid
- Cotton batting to size
- Insulated batting to size
- Thread
- Template material
- Fusible web with paper release
- Basic sewing tools and supplies

Project Notes

Read all instructions before beginning this project.

Materials and cutting lists assume 40" of usable fabric width for yardage and 20" for fat quarters.

Cutting

From green or tan tonal:

- Cut 2 (9" x 11") A rectangles.

From black solid:

- Cut 2 (2¼" by fabric width) binding strips.

Completing the Mug Rug

Refer to the Placement Diagram for positioning of pieces.

1. Referring to Raw-Edge Fusible Appliqué on page 10, prepare templates for handle, cup, rim and inside using pattern provided. Use templates to trace one of each shape on paper side of fusible web and cut out.

2. Fuse shapes to wrong side of fabrics as listed. Cut out and remove backing paper.

- Black: 1 each handle and rim
- Brown: 1 each cup and inside

3. Position all pieces on an A rectangle and fuse in place according to manufacturer's directions.

4. Using your chosen machine stitch, stitch appliqué pieces in place. Sample was stitched with a reduced straight stitch close to the edge.

5. Optional: With a water-soluble marker, write "Coffee" or "Espresso" or a message of your choice on background fabric.

6. Layer the plain A rectangle, wrong side up; insulated batting, shiny side down; cotton batting; and the appliquéd rectangle, right side up; pin-baste to hold.

7. Quilt as desired. Use free-motion quilting with contrasting thread to stitch over any writing.

Coffee
Espresso

8. Trim quilted mug rug to 8½" x 10" rectangle, centering the appliqué motif and writing.

9. To make the second mug rug, follow steps 1–8 and flip the handle template when tracing to have the coffee mug in reverse.

10. Bind referring to Quilting Basics on page 45. ●

Refreshing Mug Rugs
Placement Diagram 8½" x 10" including binding

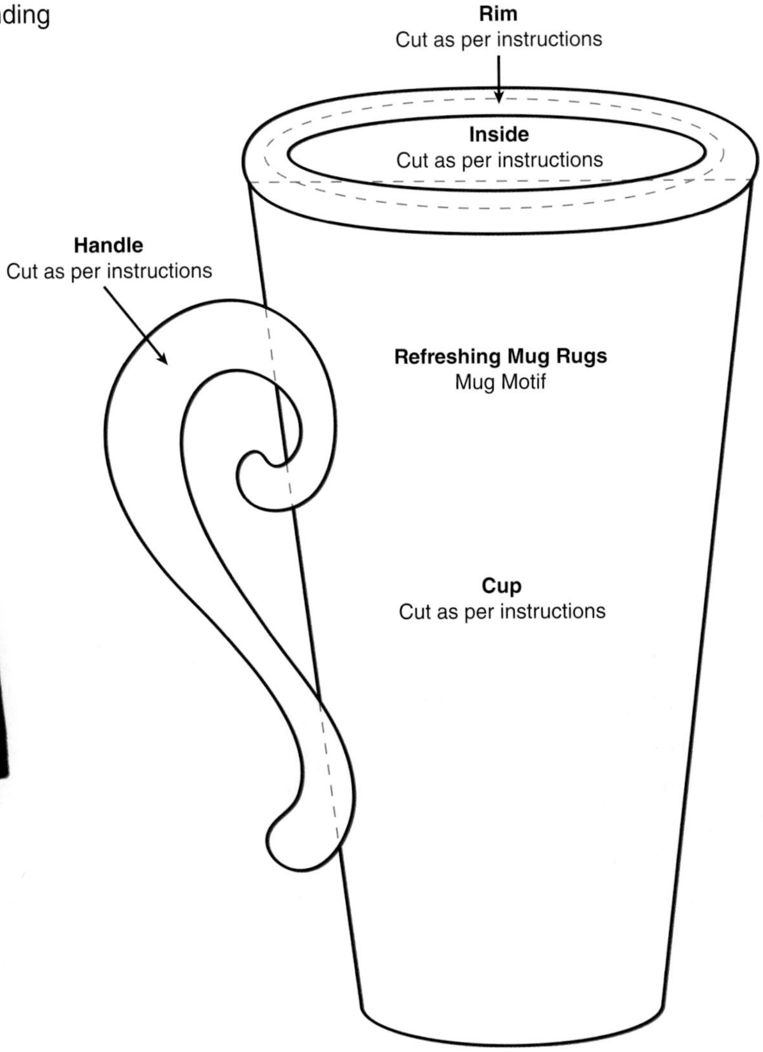

Quilting Basics

The following is a reference guide. For more information, consult a comprehensive quilting book.

Always:

- Read through the entire pattern before you begin your project.
- Purchase quality, 100 percent cotton fabrics.
- When considering prewashing, do so with ALL of the fabrics being used. Generally, prewashing is not required in quilting.
- Use ¼" seam allowance for all stitching unless otherwise instructed.
- Use a short-to-medium stitch length.
- Make sure your seams are accurate.

Quilting Tools & Supplies

- Rotary cutter and mat
- Scissors for paper and fabric
- Non-slip quilting rulers
- Marking tools
- Sewing machine
- Sewing machine feet:
  - ¼" seaming foot (for piecing)
  - Walking or even-feed foot (for piecing or quilting)
  - Darning or free-motion foot (for free-motion quilting)
- Quilting hand-sewing needles
- Straight pins
- Curved safety pins for basting
- Seam ripper
- Iron and ironing surface

Basic Techniques

Appliqué

Fusible Appliqué

All templates are reversed for use with this technique.

1. Trace the instructed number of templates ¼" apart onto the paper side of paper-backed fusible web. Cut apart the templates, leaving a margin around each, and fuse to the wrong side of the fabric following fusible web manufacturer's instructions.

2. Cut the appliqué pieces out on the traced lines, remove paper backing and fuse to the background referring to the appliqué motif given.

3. Finish appliqué raw edges with a straight, satin, blanket, zigzag or blind-hem machine stitch with matching or invisible thread.

Turned-Edge Appliqué

1. Trace the printed reversed templates onto template plastic. Flip the template over and mark as the right side.

2. Position the template, right side up, on the right side of fabric and lightly trace, spacing images ½" apart. Cut apart, leaving a ¼" margin around the traced lines.

3. Clip curves and press edges ¼" to the wrong side around the appliqué shape.

4. Referring to the appliqué motif, pin or baste appliqué shapes to the background.

5. Hand-stitch shapes in place using a blind stitch and thread to match or machine-stitch using a short blind hemstitch and either matching or invisible thread.

Borders

Most patterns give an exact size to cut borders. You may check those sizes by comparing them to the horizontal and vertical center measurements of your quilt top.

Straight Borders

1. Mark the centers of the side borders and quilt top sides.

2. Stitch borders to quilt top sides with right sides together and matching raw edges and center marks using a ¼" seam. Press seams toward borders.

3. Repeat with top and bottom border lengths.

Mitered Borders

1. Add at least twice the border width to the border lengths instructed to cut.

2. Center and sew the side borders to the quilt, beginning and ending stitching ¼" from the quilt corner and backstitching (Figure 1). Repeat with the top and bottom borders.

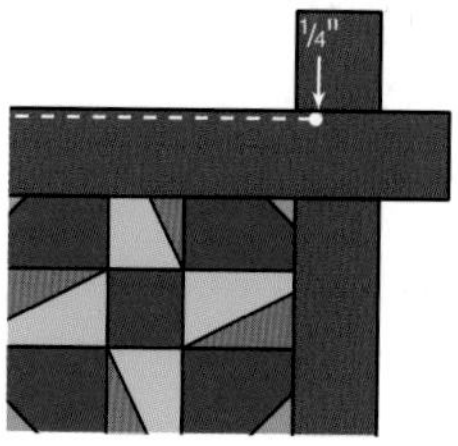

Figure 1

3. Fold and pin quilt right sides together at a 45-degree angle on one corner (Figure 2). Place a straightedge along the fold and lightly mark a line across the border ends.

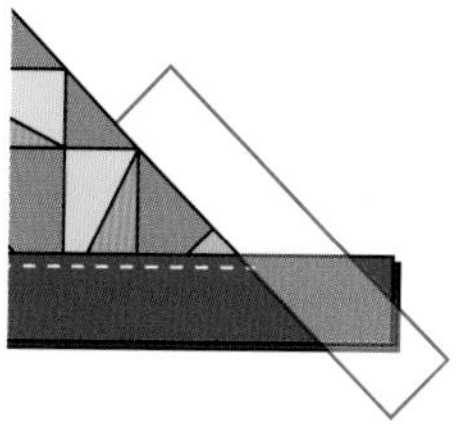

Figure 2

4. Stitch along the line, backstitching to secure. Trim seam to ¼" and press open (Figure 3).

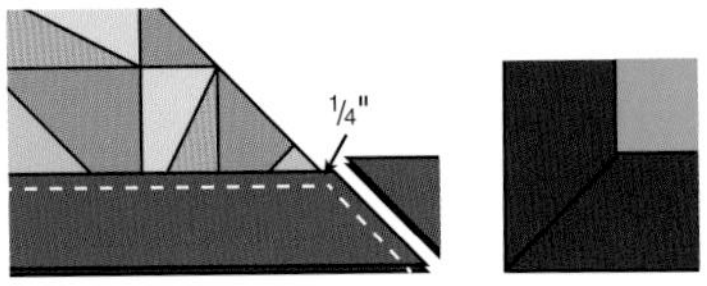

Figure 3

Quilt Backing & Batting

We suggest that you cut your backing and batting 8" larger than the finished quilt-top size. If preparing the backing from standard-width fabrics, remove the selvages and sew two or three lengths together; press seams open. If using 108"-wide fabric, trim to size on the straight grain of the fabric.

Prepare batting the same size as your backing. You can purchase prepackaged sizes or battings by the yard and trim to size.

Quilting

1. Press quilt top on both sides and trim all loose threads.

2. Make a quilt sandwich by layering the backing right side down, batting and quilt top centered right side up on flat surface and smooth out. Pin or baste layers together to hold.

3. Mark quilting design on quilt top and quilt as desired by hand or machine. ***Note:*** *If you are sending your quilt to a professional quilter, contact them for specifics about preparing your quilt for quilting.*

4. When quilting is complete, remove pins or basting. Trim batting and backing edges even with raw edges of quilt top.

Binding the Quilt

1. Join binding strips on short ends with diagonal seams to make one long strip; trim seams to ¼" and press seams open (Figure 4).

2. Fold 1" of one short end to wrong side and press. Fold the binding strip in half with wrong sides together along length, again referring to Figure 4; press.

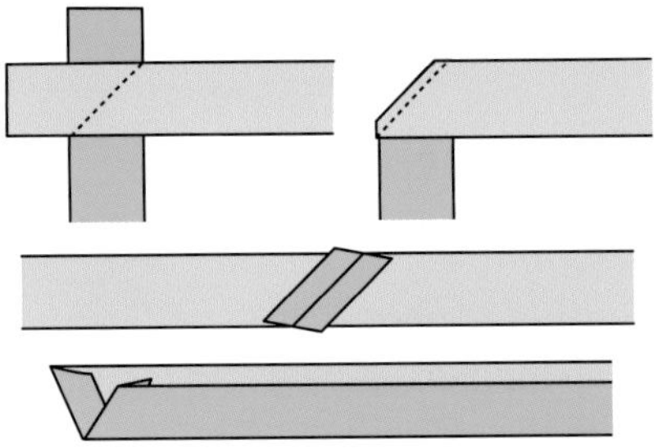

Figure 4

3. Starting about 3" from the folded short end, sew binding to quilt top edges, matching raw edges and using a ¼" seam. Stop stitching ¼" from corner and backstitch (Figure 5).

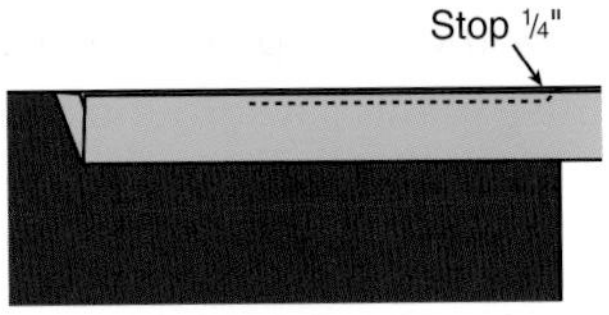

Figure 5

4. Fold binding up at a 45-degree angle to seam and then down even with quilt edges, forming a pleat at corner, referring to Figure 6.

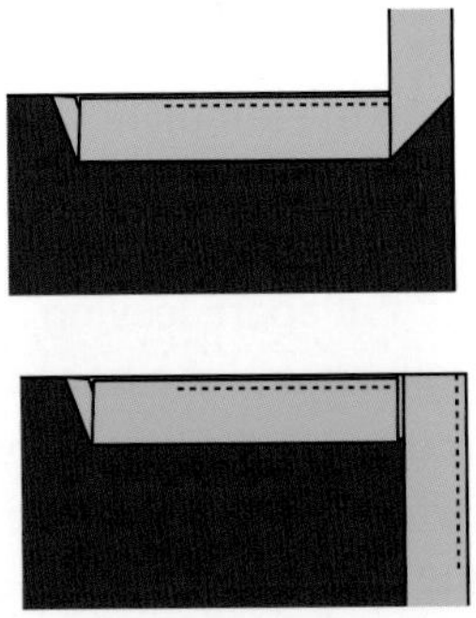

Figure 6

5. Resume stitching from corner edge as shown in Figure 6, down quilt side, backstitching ¼" from next corner. Repeat, mitering all corners, stitching to within 3" of starting point.

6. Trim binding end long enough to tuck inside starting end and complete stitching (Figure 7).

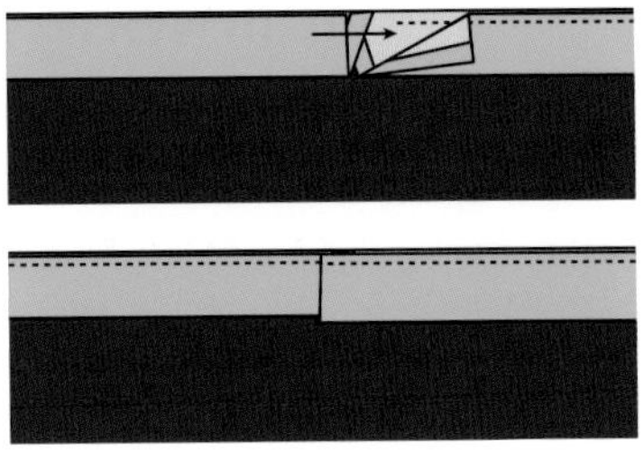

Figure 7

7. Fold binding to quilt back and stitch in place by hand or machine to complete your quilt.

Quilting Terms

- **Appliqué:** Adding fabric motifs to a foundation fabric by hand or machine (see Appliqué section of Basic Techniques).
- **Basting:** This temporarily secures layers of quilting materials together with safety pins, thread or a spray adhesive in preparation for quilting the layers.

  Use a long, straight stitch to hand- or machine-stitch one element to another holding the elements in place during construction and usually removed after construction.
- **Batting:** An insulating material made in a variety of fiber contents that is used between the quilt top and back to provide extra warmth and loft.
- **Binding:** A finishing strip of fabric sewn to the outer raw edges of a quilt to cover them.

  Straight-grain binding strips, cut on the crosswise straight grain of the fabric (see Straight & Bias Grain Lines illustration on page 47), are commonly used.

  Bias binding strips are cut at a 45-degree angle to the straight grain of the fabric. They are used when binding is being added to curved edges.

- **Block:** The basic quilting unit that is repeated to complete the quilt's design composition. Blocks can be pieced, appliquéd or solid and are usually square or rectangular in shape.
- **Border:** The frame of a quilt's central design used to visually complete the design and give the eye a place to rest.
- **Fabric Grain:** The fibers that run either parallel (lengthwise grain) or perpendicular (crosswise grain) to the fabric selvage are straight grain.

  Bias is any diagonal line between the lengthwise or crosswise grain. At these angles the fabric is less stable and stretches easily. The true bias of a woven fabric is a 45-degree angle between the lengthwise and crosswise grain lines.

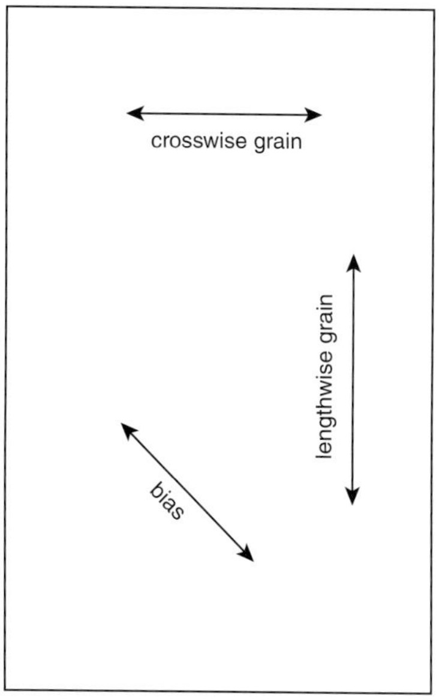

Straight & Bias Grain Lines

- **Mitered Corners:** Matching borders or turning bindings at a 45-degree angle at corners.
- **Patchwork:** A general term for the completed blocks or quilts that are made from smaller shapes sewn together.
- **Pattern:** This may refer to the design of a fabric or to the written instructions for a particular quilt design.
- **Piecing:** The act of sewing smaller pieces and/or units of a block or quilt together.

  Paper or foundation piecing is sewing fabric to a paper or cloth foundation in a certain order.

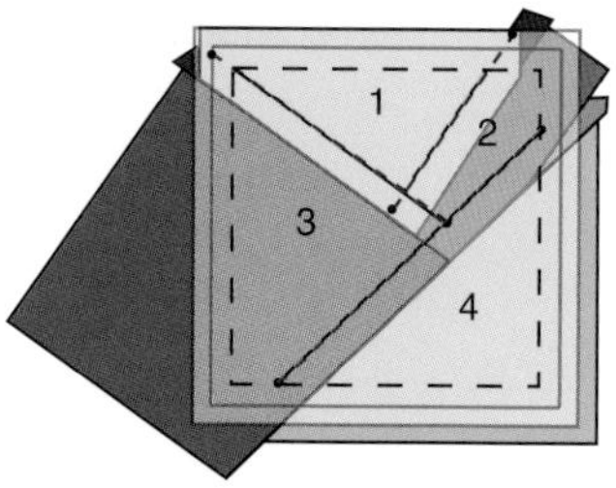

Foundation Piecing

String or chain piecing is sewing pieces together in a continuous string without clipping threads between sections.

String or Chain Piecing

- **Pressing:** Pressing is the process of placing the iron on the fabric, lifting it off the fabric and placing it down in another location to flatten seams or crease fabric without sliding the iron across the fabric.

  Quilters do not usually use steam when pressing, since it can easily distort fabric shapes.

  Generally, seam allowances are pressed toward the darker fabric in quilting so that they do not show through the lighter fabric.

  Seams are pressed in opposite directions where seams are being joined to allow seams to butt against each other and to distribute bulk.

  Seams are pressed open when multiple seams come together in one place.

  If you have a question about pressing direction, consult a comprehensive quilting guide for guidance.
- **Quilt (noun):** A sandwich of two layers of fabric with a third insulating material between them that is then stitched together with the edges covered or bound.
- **Quilt (verb):** Stitching several layers of fabric materials together with a decorative design. Stippling, crosshatch, channel, in-the-ditch, free-motion, allover and meandering are all terms for quilting designs.

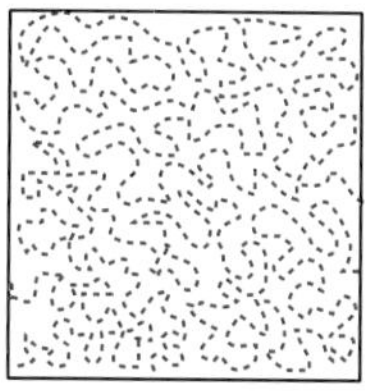

Meandering

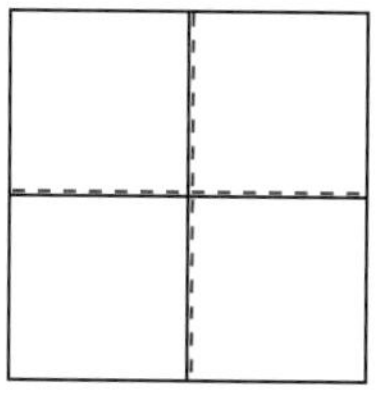

Stitch-in-the-ditch

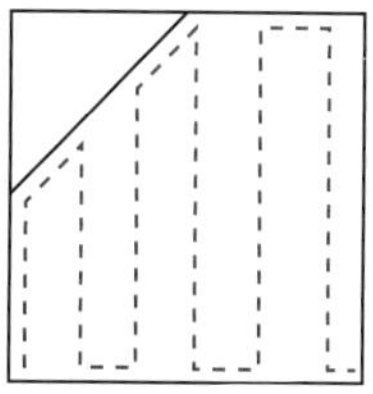

Channel

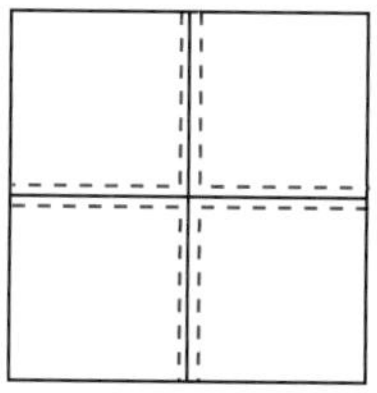

Outline

- **Quilt Sandwich:** A layer of insulating material between a quilt's top and back fabric.
- **Rotary Cutting:** Using a rotary cutting blade and straightedge to cut fabric.
- **Sashing:** Strips of fabric sewn between blocks to separate or set off the designs.
- **Subcut:** A second cutting of rotary-cut strips that makes the basic shapes used in block and quilt construction.
- **Template:** A pattern made from a sturdy material which is then used to cut shapes for patchwork and appliqué quilting.

Special Thanks

Please join us in thanking the talented designers whose work is featured in this collection.

Lyn Brown
Festival Quilt, page 15

Bev Getschel
Charm Plus, page 2
Dancing in the Rain, page12

Connie Kauffman
Crossing Lines, page 23

Nancy Walhout Recker
Porch Swing, page 6
Sunset at the Beach, page 39

Nancy Scott
Charming Stars & Pinwheels, page 18
Linear Quilt, page 32

Sharon Tucker
Charming Stars, page 28

Carolyn S. Vagts
Butterfly Trio Hot Pads, page 35
Refreshing Mug Rugs, page 42

Supplies

We would like to thank the following manufacturers who provided materials to our designers to make sample projects for this book.

Charm Plus, page 2: Sparrow charm pack and fabrics from Hoffman California Fabrics; American Spirit 70/30 batting from Fairfield.

Porch Swing, page 6: Acreage charm pack and fabric from Moda.

Dancing in the Rain, page 12: Desert Bloom charm pack from Moda; American Spirit 70/30 batting from Fairfield.

Festival Quilt, page 15: Cockatiel charm pack from Hoffman California Fabrics.

Charming Stars & Pinwheels, page 18: Strawberry Fields Revisited charm pack by Joanna Figueroa, Fig Tree & Co., from Moda; digital quilting pattern from TK Quilting & Design.

Crossing Lines, page 23: Drizzle charm pack and fabric from Island Batik; Warm Blend batting from The Warm Company; cotton 40 wt. thread from Aurifil.

Linear Quilt, page 32: Sevilla Mellow Yellows by Andrea Komninos from Benartex Contempo Studio; digital quilting pattern from TK Quilting & Design.

Sunset at the Beach, page 39: Wild Waves charm pack and fabric from Moda.

Annie's®
Just Charm Quilts is published by Annie's, 306 East Parr Road, Berne, IN 46711. Printed in USA.

RETAIL STORES: If you would like to carry this publication or any other Annie's publications, visit AnniesWSL.com.

ISBN: 978-1-59012-748-3

3 4 5 6 7 8 9